Spiritual Rhymes (On Recogr

In the name of God,
compassionate and merciful

1

IF RUMI WAS ENGLISH ...

SPIRITUAL RHYMES

VOLUME 1

ON RECOGNITION OF SOUL & EGO

TRANSLATED BY AMIN HEDAYAT

**I have been whimpering to everyone
As a mate of a sad or happy one**

**Each befriended me with their own thought
My inner mystiques were never sought**

Rumi

Forty years of my life passed without anyone truly and perfectly seeking my inner mystiques. Although anyone you meet in your life somehow adds to your knowledge, but there is always that special one that discovers and nourishes your inner mystiques, and helps you to become a better version of yourself and wiser human being. For my life, that most significant one is my wife, Mahsa, whose place is always warm in my heart and is a great source of support and inspiration for me in general and specifically in translating Rum's poetry.

Smile since my world is in that beautiful grin

Smile such that I see that beauty coming from within

me

Contents

یک دست جام باده و یک دست زلف یار
رقصی چنین میانهٔ میدانم آرزوست

PREFACE by the Interpreter

It was just another repetitive day at work; it was another Monday, and it was mundane again. Sitting behind my desktop, I was struggling to find an incentive to push through my daily tasks. In front of me on my screen, there was again bunch of characters and numbers, which we programmers simply call it code. Knowing that a five-figure paycheck will soon flow into my bank account was not encouraging anymore to deal with these conventional characters. And for sure an eventfully spent weekend was not enticing enough as there were all the same old events that I had since I moved to Canada when I was 21.

Surprisingly, I was becoming less interested in social gatherings, parties, night clubs or even making more friends. Few years ago, these still sounded very pleasing to me, but always that "Something is missing" quote would run through my conscience. I began to discern that my glamorous western lifestyle was becoming too much of meaningless numbers, statuses, and materialistic gains. For guys, it was all about making more money here and there to buy themselves more entourage and social status and rationally underneath it all, having more sexual intercourse! And for most girls I knew was all about buying more cosmetics and sexy dress to look more sexually attractive to hunt guys with higher statuses.

I even had friends who had an actual written list of women they slept with. And all they could teach you about in their conversations was showing you how to fool girls into sleeping with you, or what kind of cars to buy next when they make and save more money. However, I had them all: a six-figure salary, a Mercedes, and a pool of girls in my entourage. It was about time for something more meaningful: the real purpose of life!

Dealing with my mid-age crisis, I started seeing my life coach again. In one of the sessions, she basically assessed me just as a person so sick of the too-materialistic and individualistic way of Western life style. She suggested me that I should have a trip to my home country and had a rest there beside my family and relatives to be a while away from the hurly-burly of Canadian life.

It had been also a while that strangely, I was incidentally seeing some repetitious digits on my phone time, car plates, etc. which I ignored in the beginning, but later having a mentality of a programming analyst, I started researching this on the web to find out that not only so many others are experiencing them but they did also even make themselves a newly coined word as "angel numbers", and there are even books about them!

What I intuitionally realized from all that research finally was that I need to make myself a new beginning, a different path, and a new way of life. However, I had a hard time figuring out how and where to start. I don't want to make a big deal of these angel numbers for myself and others, but through my research I even realized that they would even talk back to me and would reply to me through numbers if I attentively called the angels in my mind. Therefore, I asked them about whether to quit my job and spend sometime in Iran. Miraculously enough, they did answer me at a time that I expect it the least like usual, with numbers that meant yes to me. I decided to quit my job and have a long journey to my home country, Iran, while the future seemed so unknown.

During my second stay in Iran in the peak of coronavirus era, some events lead to another to propel me to visit Mashhad which is a religious city in Iran. In Mashhad, my girlfriend (my present beloved wife), knowing my enthusiasm for history and literature, took me to visit Ferdowsi tomb. Over there, I saw a shop selling the works of famous Iranian poets in form of CDs or desktop applications. To satisfy my eagerness for Iranian poetry, I bought couple of packages containing Ferdowsi's, Hafez', and Rumi's poems with commentary and research tools.

I am not sure why but even though I enjoyed reading Hafez' and Ferdowsi's poems, The poems of *Masnavi[1] Manavi* composed by Rumi got through me the most since its very beginning:

Listen to this reed as it sings,

And as it complains of partings.

Since they cut me out of the reedbed,

So many have wailed in my ballad.

I need a heart, who felt the parting,

To relate the tension of longing.

Each soul, left far from its origin,

Seeks again its days of belonging.

I have been whimpering to everyone

As a mate of a sad or happy one;

Each befriended me with their own thought;

   My inner mystiques were never sought.

After reading the verse 5, I just intuitively discerned that, that might be the missing part: the never-sought inner mystique. We humans rarely try to seek and nourish our inner mystiques in ourselves or others; that might be what was missing in my life. Verse 3 also clearly states that humans are experiencing lost connections, and they are instinctively trying to go back to them while they're staged far from them through life. Life is an implicit struggle to find back the genesis, we belong to, where our soul can peacefully rest at last.

After reading more Rumi's poems and studying its commentaries here and there, I realized his translated poems in English on the web or books never clearly and deeply convey the message that Rumi really meant to covey. Therefore, it came to my mind that perhaps by translating and interpreting Rumi's poems into simple English, not only I can give a meaning and purpose to my own life, but also, I can assist a whole lot of people who lost their spiritual connections to universe and were left far from meaningful

---

[1] Masnavi in general is a form of Farsi (official language of Iranians) poem in which every verse has two rhymed couplets meaning that the last word of every couplet in a verse rhymes.

aspects of life. Likewise, I decided to use plain simple English as English is a pretty well globally spoken language, but not everyone can easily read and understand works in English literature such as those written by Shakespeare.

Therefore, I thank the Lord for giving me the gift and honor of translating one of the most valuable books of the world in the category of spiritual teachings from Persian (Farsi) to English. This is the 1st book of mine in the series of my translations of *Masnavi Manavi* [2] which is in fact the interpretation on those sections of Rumi's Masnavi's book 1 that spans from its original introduction to the end of the Jew King stories.

Most of the English translations of Rumi's poems in the current market are from his two major poetic works:

- One is *The Works of Shams of Tabriz* [3], named in honor of Rumi's mystic master: *Shams Tabrizi*,
- Second is Masnavi Manavi or Spiritual rhyming Couplets.

Rumi Started authoring the first one in the earlier stage of his life; perhaps when he was about 40, but it did last as long as Rumi aged. These poems are in form of *Ghazal* which is a specific form of Iranian (Persian) poem, and they mainly describe the elevated mystic moods of Rumi. Most commentators believe that these poems are just a spontaneous biproduct of Rumi's mystic connection to divine love. Some western readers or scholars wrongfully described Rumi's Poems in Shams' Works as amatory; however, they don't realize that these poems of Rumi are only amatory in the surface, but it does in its depth depicts his mystical spiritual connection to divine love.

The work on his other collection of poems, in form of *Masnavi* or rhyming couplets, started when he was 54, at the age when he mastered all his mystic knowledge of divine love. Therefore, with the suggestion of one of his disciples, he began authoring the Masnavi to teach the secrets of divine love and true spirituality to his followers. As a result, if a reader decides to learn essentials of spirituality and the essence of life, they need to read Masnavi.

---

[2] From now on in this book, we use the word "the Masnavi" as a referral to Masnavi Manavi of Rumi.

[3] From now on in this book, we use the word "Shams' Works" as a referral to *The Works of Shams of Tabriz*.

It is a very accurate assessment if we consider Rumi in Shams' Works a devotee poet but in Masnavi a teacher poet. While Shams' Works were perhaps composed in private spiritual times of Rumi, or during his sessions of *Sama*[4] music and dance with other Sufis, Masnavi was composed during his educational sermons and lessons. And of course, in both cases and specially the latter, the poems were mostly scripted by his disciples while Rumi was just verbally revealing them.

Unfortunately, though, most of the Masnavi's translations in today's market of western world are very poor and far from the meanings that Rumi has intended to convey to his reader. Therefore, I felt the need in our today's materialistic world to correctly and comprehensively translate and interpret Rumi's Masnavi with the help of the almighty Lord.

A Bit About Me

I was born in Iran and lived there till I was 21. I moved to Canada in the middle of my post secondary education in Software Engineering in Shahid Beheshti University and I have lived in Vancouver for almost 20 years. After passing several Business Communications courses, I studied Computer Systems Technology at BCIT, and worked for several known companies such as Sita, ABB, and Boeing in Vancouver where I had to compose several technical writings on a daily basis to document my part of or sometimes others' parts of work.

I am also an enthusiast of Persian spiritual poetry and read several Iranian poems daily. I am also interested in reading the works of some American poet like *Henry Wadsworth Longfellow*.

Translation Style in This Book

The translation of Rumi's Masnavi in this book is rhymed and is in form of poem, and it is not intended to be a word by word or even verse by verse translation of the whole Masnavi. However, the main goal of translation in this book is to convey all the key points of the spiritual teachings of Rumi's Masnavi. Moreover, the translation is also rhymed like the original Iranian

---

[4] Sama is a Sufi celebration in which Sufis sing prayers to praise God while playing musical instruments and perform a whirling dance usually with right hand up with palm and fingers pointing to the sky and with the other hand diagonally down with palm and fingers pointing to the earth.

poem to make it more attractive and memorable to the readers and of course without compromising any of the original intended meanings.

Rumi often tried to clarify his spiritual message in multiple examples which may sound a bit unnecessary to an intelligent reader, although Rumi's examples are very elaborative and were cleverly synthesized to elaborate the main points of the topic. However, to respect the narrow time of readers of today's world, I decided to summarize or skip some of Rumi's verses in this book. However, I did pay all my attention throughout the translation to not deviate or omit any essential meanings Rumi was trying to teach to his readers.

Moreover, there are some terminologies used in this book that the reader may need to realize its meaning or spiritual semantics. Words like soul, heart, and spirit, each owns a separate signification in Rumi's teachings. I tried to explain the meaning of these words specifically in footnotes or more generally in the interpretive section after the story.

One of the subtle changes I made in my translation compared to the original is that I sometimes used the pronoun "we" rather than "you", or "let's" rather than mere imperative verbs which was widely used in the original book since I thought using "we" may make the text more friendly especially to younger generations. Nobody likes to constantly hear "you should do this and that" in the form of imperative sentences; nevertheless, nobody should mind receiving advising sentences from a well-known knowledgeable saint like Rumi.

My usage of pronouns in this text also differs a bit from the common spoken English. Whenever the person, talked about, is not clearly masculine or feminine and rather is just a generic individual, I used "They", "Theirs", "Them" instead of "He", "His", or "Him" or the equivalent feminine pronouns of those. I have likewise established a new way of referring to the almighty Lord by using pronouns "It" and "Its" (capitalized for respect and distinction) as the essence of God is epicene, and using "He", "His", or "Him" can be disputable by feminine readers, and "They" or "Theirs" will defy the oneness and purity of the Deity.

Rumi being a proficient writer uses a lot of examples, proverbs and figures of speech in his poems to more clearly project his spiritual concepts to the reader. Of course, the examples he used made a perfect sense when he was composing his book almost 6 centuries ago for Persian readers, and some still do; nevertheless, I tried my best to modernize his examples when necessary and replace his Persian proverbs, idioms, or figures of speech with the equivalent English ones to make it more understandable for millennial readers.

Prologue

In the name of God, compassionate and merciful

This is the book of Masnavi[5], which is the very roots of the religion[6] to reveal the mysteries of [spiritual] attainment and certitude, and it's the greatest science of God, clearest laws of God, and the most evident argumentation of God.

"An example of Its light is a lantern in which there is a lamp" [7] that illuminates the world brighter than dawn, and it is the heart of the heavens, having springs and gardens. One of these springs is called "Salsabeel" [8] among the wayfarers of this path, and nobles owning dignity and generosity

---

[5] Rhymed poems in Iranian (Persian) poetry.

[6] It's very interesting that Rumi doesn't mention the name of the religion here! We can assume that Rumi means Islam by the word "religion" here, but even though Islamic teachings has a very important role in Rumi's thoughts and discoveries, we will further realize that Rumi considers all different religions as a tool to reach this one religion of spirituality.

[7] Quoted from Quran, Surah an-Noor (light), verse 35, (24:35).

[8] A spring in paradise, named in Quran, in Surah Insan (human), verse 18, (76:18).

would give it (the book of Masnavi) the finest grade and would find it pleasantly soothing. Therein, the righteous eat and drink, and thereby the broad-minded are cheered and rejoiced; an example of that is the Nile River which is a pleasant drink to the tolerant and a regret to the pharaohs and infidels;[9] and as Great God said: *"Many are misled by it, and many are guided [to the divine truth] by it."* [10]

It (the book of Masnavi) is [moreover], the cure for [hurt] hearts, the polish of sorrows, the interpreter of the Quran, the expansion of blessings, and the purifier of ethics *"with the help of noble righteous scribes"* [11] who prevent *"others from touching it except the impeccable"*; [12] and *"it (the Quran or the Masnavi) is a revelation from the Lord of the universe"*, that *"no falsification can enter it from any side"* [13] since God observes and watches over it, and *"he is the best guardian and the most merciful of all."* [14] There are also other titles that the Great God has assigned to it (the Quran or the Masnavi); however, we summarized them here to a few, as the few words can describe a lot of concepts as you may know by a handful the whole sack.

This delicate man, in need of mercy from the Great God, Mohammad, son of Mohammad, son of Mohammad, son of al-Hossain, of [the city of] Balkh,[15] may God accept [this book] from him, says: "I strived to expand

---

[9] This is a referral to a quranic and biblical story of Moses and Israelites traveling back to their homeland after pharaoh's agreement. Nevertheless, when the Israelites were close to the Nile River, the pharaoh changed his mind and sent his troops on chariots to ensue them. Moses then splits the river using his magical staff to help the Israelites cross to the other side of the sea; however, by the time that Egyptian soldiers try to use the same path to ensue the Israelites, the sea waves remerged and drowned the pharaoh's soldiers.

[10] Quoted from Quran, Surah Al-Baqarah (cow), verse 26, (2:26).

[11] Quoted from Quran, Surah 'Abasa (He Frowned), verses 15-16, (80:15-16).

[12] Quoted from Quran, Surah Al-Waqi'ah (The Inevitable Incident), verses 79-80, (56:79-80).

[13] Quoted from Quran, Surah Fussilat (It Detailed), verse 42, (41:42).

[14] Quoted from Quran, Surah Yusuf (Joseph), verse 64, (12:64).

[15] Muslims in the past used to use their father's names and the name of the city they were born in, instead of our current last names to be more distinguished.

this set of rhymed poems which consists of wonderful, scarce and select discourses, precious tips, and the doctrine of ascetics; and it is the [spiritual] garden of devotees with a few basics [of spiritual life], but also with a lot of meanings."

I am doing this at the request of my master, supporter, and trustworthy person, holding the spirit of my body, who is also my substitute for today or tomorrow. He is a senior icon of mystics, a leader for followers of the right path and [spiritual] certitude, the savior of the people, a confidant of hearts and consciences, the God's trust among Its creatures, and an elite habitant of Its wonderland. He is also well aware of God's instructions to his prophet, and of Its mysteries shared with Its chosen ones. He is, moreover, a key to celestial and terrestrial treasuries, a possessor of virtues, a sharp representative of truth and religion.

His name is Hassan, son of Mohammad, son of Hassan, known as Ibn Akhi Turk, the Abu Yazíd of the time, the Junaid of the era, born in a sincere progeny, may God be well-pleased with him and with them! He is originally from Urmia, and he is related to the veteran honorable for having said: "In the evening, I slept as a Kurd, but in the morning, I woke up as an Arab!";[16] may God make his and his successors' spirit sacred! How awesome is the ancestor and how great is the successor! He is from a lineage upon which the Sun has cast its cape of light on, and his fame is so brilliant that dims the beams of the stars.

Their courtyard is always open like a fortune giving center to governors' children, and as a destination to circumambulate for delegations of virtue to reach their [spiritual] wishes; and may it never cease to be as such till a star rises and a sun blooms so that it becomes a sanctuary for the godly spiritual celestial heavenly enlightened ones who possess (mystical) insights, for the silent observers, the present absentees, the rags-wearing kings[17], the nobles of tribes, the possessors of virtues, and the illuminators of [divine] testaments. Amen O Lord of all universes! And that is a prayer that won't be rejected as it applies to all varieties of species.

---

[16] Implying that nationality is not important in Islam and Sufism

[17] The rags-wearing kings are in fact Sufis as they were used to being given a run-down woolen robe by their master to wear as a recognition of their sincerity and devotion and likewise as a sign to their spiritual non-materialistic life.

Worship be to God who is no one's own, and may God bless our master, Mohammad, and his pure and virtuous family and ancestry; and *"God by itself suffices us, and what a guardian he is!"* [18]

---

[18] Quoted from Quran, Surah Al-Imran (Imran's lineage), verse 173, (3:173).

بشنو این نی چون حکایت می‌کند
از جدایی‌ها شکایت می‌کند

Listen to this reed as it sings

And as it complains of partings

Notes of Reed-flute

Listen to this reed[19] as it sings,
And as it complains of partings[20].

---

[19] Reed Flute, a musical instrument. The reed here represents a perfect human soul who is empty of arrogance, egotism, and sins as the reed itself is as well empty inside, and by blowing in it you can produce meaningful spiritual songs! It is widely believed by most interpreters of the Masnavi that reed here is actually Rumi himself.

[20] We can specify two interpretations for the word "partings" here; first is the lost connections or specifically the separation of the human soul or spirit from its origin which is the divine connection; second is pointing to all trivial and nominal separations among the people in this world, mainly caused by labels of religions and nationalities, even though they all do have one origin which is the divinity.

21

Since they cut me out of the reedbed[21],

> So many have wailed in my ballad.[22]

I need a heart ruptured by parting

> To relate the tensions of longing[23].[24]

Each soul left far from its origin

> Seeks again its days of belonging.[25]

---

[21] Reedbed represents the spiritual world that Rumi believes the human soul or spirit has separated from, i.e., heaven. This verse, is also a very tacit referral to Adam an Eve story in which they got expelled from heaven after they ate the forbidden fruit.

[22] Rumi claims here that his spiritual wisdom (ballad) contains other people's stories (whether mystic or ordinary) too; meaning that by hearing and analyzing other people's life stories, Rumi realized what is mainly missing from people's lives to make deep connection to the real meaning of life and taste the real happiness. Therefore now, he (the reed) is going to play us his spiritual song (wisdom) including lessons from many people's lives not just his. This verse also implicitly states that spiritual wisdom is a collaborative knowledge, and anyone can absorb it if paying enough heed.

[23] Longing for another connection (mainly to divinity).

[24] By this verse, Rumi is selecting his real audience, and they are who tasted the bitterness of losing a connection or relation, and subsequently they yearned for that connection to happen again.

[25] Any soul who was left distant from their prior connection (mainly divine connection) will seek to establish that connection again, so that they can again feel that sense of belonging to that connection or relation.

Of longing

the tensions

To relate

by Parting

Ruptured

Heart

I need a

شرح درد اشتیاق

تا بگویم

از فراق

سینه خواهم شرحه شرحه

I have been whimpering to everyone

    As a mate of a sad or happy one;[26]

Each befriended me with their own thought;

    My inner mystiques were never sought.[27]

My mystiques aren't too far from my lament;

    There is just not enough enlightenment.[28]

---

[26] Rumi is expressing here that he has been trying so hard to explain his findings (partings of human souls from divinity and possibly other Sufistic findings) to all sorts of people, hoping that someone finally would understand and make connections with him and his discoveries. This verse also implicitly specifies that on his path to gain his spiritual wisdom, Rumi socialized with all sorts of people (sad or happy) believing everyone has a story to tell that can be educational to others.

[27] Even though Rumi tried so hard to discuss his wisdom with others, not many really made the sufficient connection to him and his spiritual discoveries (inner mystiques) from the bottom of their heart because most people approached him and his wisdom from their own point of view causing them to not deeply find out the core of his spiritual teachings, or perhaps they just befriended him for their own benefit. Therefore, it's really important to lose all our prior perceptions and viewpoints to profoundly comprehend Rumi's wisdom.

[28] Rumi's (the reed's) mystiques (spiritual mysteries) are discoverable and perceptible through his words (the reed's lament). This is also one of the essentials of modern psychology; an individual's words and tune of talk can determine their personality and also reveal their thoughts.

Body and soul aren't concealed from each other,

But the former isn't ruled to see the latter.[29]

The reed's song is out of spark[30], not air;

One without this spark should take a powder[31][32]

The spark of love goes into the canes;

It's the simmer of love, the wine gains.

The reed backs all whose hearts were slain;

All veils were torn by its song strain[33].[34]

---

[29] Rumi is giving an example of why his mystic secrets and findings are not perceptible enough to the ordinary. Human soul and body, though belonging to separate worlds, can perceive each other; especially we or our body can comprehend our soul if we try hard enough to lessen our materialistic attachments. However, the big problem is that in this world our body's senses are not allowed to directly and physically sense our soul or spirit resulting in denying or not clearly understanding the religious or mystic (Sufistic) significations including soul, spirit, etc.

[30] It represents the spark of divine love that can burn a human soul and spark a new beginning which is realizing the meaning and philosophy of life.

[31] "To take a powder" means to depart quickly from a difficult situation.

[32] In this verse, Rumi is implicitly warning us that the journey to gain spiritual wisdom is a difficult one, and he is again filtering his audience similar to the verse "*I need a heart ruptured by parting...*".

[33] Strain is a damaging or penetrating force.

[34] The reed sympathizes with anyone whose heart is harshly broken and who is sick and tired of their worldly attachments and obsessions (veils), and the reed's song (Rumi's teachings and findings) can heal them by cutting through the human ego and greed (veils) and eventually can uncover their inner mystiques and the mysteries of the universe by its penetrating force (the strain of reed's song).

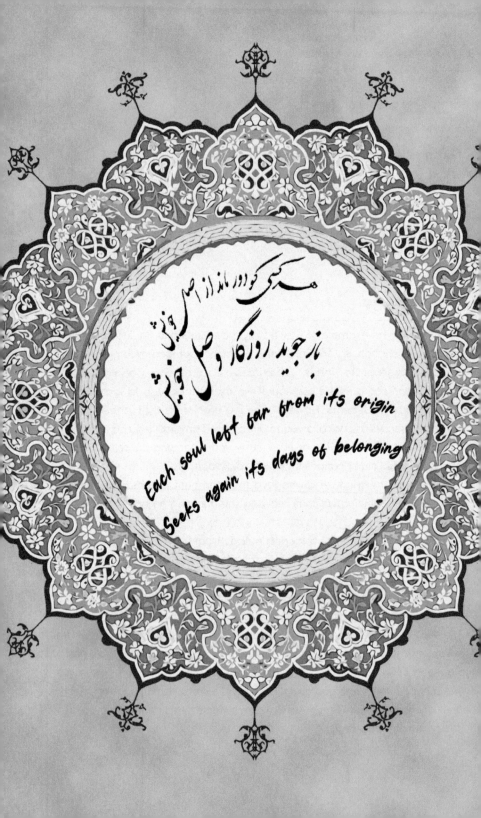

هر کسی کو دور ماند از اصل خویش
باز جوید روزگار وصل خویش

Each soul left far from its origin
Seeks again its days of belonging

No one's seen a poison and elixir like this reed;[35]

    No one's been affectionate and eager like this reed.

The reed tells the tale of a stormy tour

    And tells the story of insane amour! [36]

Realizing this wit needs no perception

    As the ear listens straight to a new lesson. [37]

---

[35] The effect of reed's songs or Rumi's teachings can be two-sided; they can be harmful like a poison to ones who are drowned in their corporal needs, but also very magically beneficial like an elixir to the life of the ones who have reduced their temporal attachments.

[36] The path to comprehension of divine truth, i.e., the spiritual way, is not easy at all but also turbulent! However, this path is full of sparkling divine love.

[37] To deeply realize Rumi's teachings, all your previous assumptions, perceptions, and knowledge must be let go!

Our grieves impaired our every morning!

Days and nights passed with too much mourning![38]

---

[38] The tension and grief of longing for connection with divinity is a daily matter! Most interpreters of Masnavi think that here Rumi is still talking about the struggle and burden you have to go through in a spiritual journey to reach its top level. Their reason is that this verse might just be shadowing the couplet *"The reed tells the story of a stormy tour"*. Therefore, they think "our grieves" in this verse are referring to the burden and struggle that the wayfarers of the spiritual journey have to undertake. However, one may argue that this verse conveys too much of a negative meaning to the reader to be pointing to the burden of the spiritual journey as spirituality in the end has to elevate your soul and make you a happier person. Therefore, I believe "our grieves", here, are pointing to the grieves that we, humans, in general, have caused ourselves because of not completely and accurately recognizing ourselves, the universe, and the real meaning of life. The evidence of this idea is the previous verse in which Rumi asked us to dump all our previous assumptions and knowledge. Subsequently, in this verse, he is giving us a reason into why he has just asked us so, and that's because whatever actions and practices that we humans have adopted based on our current understandings are wrong and are the cause of our current grieves that we are still even facing in the today's world.

No regret if many days are gone

    As long as my holy love hangs on!

Only the fish stay in the river of love!

    One lingers behind without a tear of love! [39]

The raw won't savvy the wise,

    So the talk should be concise:

Break out of your greed's prison and be free!

    How long will you be chained to luxury?!

How much of the ocean can fit in a pitcher?

    How many pitchers do you need for one dinner? [40]

---

[39] Only the fish, representing the real lovers of divine path, stay in the river of divine love because the fish critically need water to live at all times, as opposed to others needing water just to satisfy their thirst and then getting away from it. The same as the fish, real lovers always need to satisfy themselves with the love of Deity at all times unlike others that mind god only occasionally. Moreover, if we stay away from the river of divine love and don't receive any drop from this river, we will cut our spiritual feed and will fail to make any progress spiritually

[40] Rumi here is analogizing the amount of human materialistic needs to the amount of water that can fit only in one pitcher used for one dinner; saying that human materialistic needs are really limited, and anything more than that is useless greedy effort.

The greedy pitcher never gets full.

  The oyster gets pearls if it's grateful.[41]

People, whose clothes[42] got torn for love,

  Were also cleansed from greed and flaw.

O' Our mind-blowing love! Please be joyous!

  You are the doctor of any sickness.

You're the pill to egomania and selfishness!

  You're the mentor of corporal and mental wellness!

---

[41] In ancient Iran (also known as Persia), they used to believe that when it rains, oysters move up to the surface of the ocean and then open to receive a few raindrops and then go back to the bottom of the ocean to produce pearls. Therefore, Rumi is using this example to illustrate how rewarding the trait of gratitude is. Pearls going back to the bottom is an analogy of them being not greedy for receiving more raindrops and thereby being more grateful of receiving just a few raindrops. Notice that they used to believe the oysters have to go back to the bottom of ocean to be able to generate pearls.

[42] Again, clothes are a representation of materialistic attachments which need to be torn to keep a lid on an obsessive greed, and that will eventually help us to stay away from sins and flaws.

The reason that Rumi is using torn clothes in the first couplet is that back in the day, Sufis used to wear worn and torn clothes in order to achieve two goals: One was to practice their detachment from corporal interests and thereby lowering the degree of their greed, and the other was to practice their independence form people's words and thoughts about them. They used to just show up here and there in public wearing those rundown clothes, and obviously, they would notice that people are pointing them out and talking about them, but they would practice to not care about that.

Out of love, soil touched the skies! [43]

    Love dances the mounts and highs! [44]

Love inspired Mount Sinai[45] in the oasis.

    The love in the mount then sedated Moses![46]

---

[43] Pointing to the ascension of Mohammad and Jesus to heaven as they had a body made out of the earth just like us.

[44] Pointing to the quake of Mount Sinai that is the principal site of divine revelation and where God is claimed to have appeared to Moses and given him the Ten Commandments.

[45] Mount Sinai is where the Ten Commandments were revealed to Moses according to both Bible and Quran. In addition, in Surah Al-A'raf (7:143) of The Quran is mentioned that on this mountain Moses asked God to reveal Itself visually to him. God responds that you will never able to see me, but if this mount stands still under me, you will be able to see me. However, when God tried to reveal Itself on Mount Sinai, this mount quakes and causes Moses to faint.

[46] So here Rumi is teaching us two major features of divine love:

- Divine love is so powerful and penetrating that it can even affect an inanimate object like a pile of stones and soil like Mount Sinai. Therefore, divine love is so effective that can have a positive impact even on the stone-hearted people.
- Divine love is easily transferable that can flow from any entity to any other entity, or from any soul to any other, like the divine love in Mount Sinai that was transferred to Moses and sedated him. Thus, by this verse, Rumi is encouraging us to try to identify and receive the divine love in every object, entity, or phenomenon in the universe, and also share the love inside us with the universe.

If your lips truly touch the reed's,

    It will bring you lots of good reads! [47]

When someone loses their chummy buddies,

    They get mute with too many melodies.[48]

When the roses in the garden are withered

    You do not hear the trill of any songbird.[49]

It's all the beloved[50] and it's eternal,

    But the lover's[51] just a covering mortal! [52]

When the lover lacks the beloved's caring love,

---

[47] Rumi asks the readers to be a decent companion to this reed (Rumi's wisdom in the Masnavi) and to start harmonizing their conscience with his wisdom by blowing in this reed with their lips so that the reed (Rumi) sings and tells them enlightening stories. So primarily Rumi wants you to put your heart and soul into reading the Masnavi, so you can actually benefit from it.

[48] This verse sounds very simple on the surface, but it, in fact, completes the meaning of the previous verse, and what it deeply means is that the same way that Rumi was able to make his deep and mystic connections to divine love to be able to spiritually sense and hear divine mysteries, you have to also make close friendship with divine love or Rumi's wisdom to be able to hear mystical enlightening stories; otherwise divine wisdom will be just like a human who lost all his close friends and (s)he's got no one to tell his illuminating stories.

[49] A Sufi or mystic will teach his findings only to people who are honestly interested in spiritual beliefs the same way that a songbird sings only to beautiful roses in a garden.

[50] God

[51] Someone who believes in God and loves to take on the spiritual journey; a mystic newbie.

[52] Here Rumi is simply telling the enthusiasts of the spiritual way that it's only their ego or their body (covering mortal) that makes a distance between them and the almighty God.

(S)He is like a wingless and featherless dove.[53]

Do we know how to move around

    If its light doesn't brighten the ground? [54]

Love wants to set this secret free outright;

    Your soul must mirror the beloved's light!

Do you know why our soul isn't a mirror?

    Because the dirt of sin makes it unclear![55]

Now, the following story should be listened to

    As it really gives human life a review.

---

[53] When the lovers lose the support and caring love of God, they will fail to fly their spiritual journey as if they lost their feather. We have to notice that Rumi here is pointing to the God's special love towards his real lovers; otherwise, God will always shine Its general love on all Its creatures.

The concepts of God's special love and general love is derived from the starting sentence of the Quran, or rather any chapter in Quran, which is "*bi-sm-i llāh-i r-raḥmān-i r-raḥīm*" often translated as "in the name of God, compassionate and merciful". The keywords, here, are *raḥmān,* and *raḥīm,* and as pointed by most Islamic interpreters, the former points to God's love as in its general form covering all creatures with no exception; on the other hand, the latter points to God's love in its more specific amd caring form covering only God's special creatures who obey him and do good deeds.

[54] A poetic example illustrating that the light of God (God's love and attention) is needed for the lovers of the spiritual path to truly and safely reach their target.

[55] If you want true inner (intuitive) guidance in spiritual journey, your soul must be free of egoistic sins and greedy desires. That way you can truly absorb and reflect the God's special love and illuminate your own spiritual path and others'. Otherwise, the dirt of sin makes your soul dirty and it won't be able to completely and correctly absorb and reflect the divine love.

روزها، گر رفت، گو رو، باک نیست!

NO REGRET IF MANY DAYS ARE GONE !

تو بمان، ای آنکه چون تو پاک نیست !

AS LONG AS MY HOLY LOVE HANGS ON !

King Falling in Love with a Maid[56]

Once upon a time, there was a king of majesty,

Who was the head of both religion and sovereignty! [57]

One day, he goes hunting on his horse

With his courtiers trailing on the course.

---

[56] This story is layered and is a love story only on its surface, but deeply each character is a symbol of a philosophical/spiritual entity. A comprehensive commentary of the story follows the story.

[57] The king in this story represents in general the human spirit which constantly tries hard to protect and nurture human soul (later represented by the maid). Like the king, the human spirit has tendencies to conquer both spiritual and temporal worlds.

36

The king saw a cute maid on the way,

    And lost his heart to her all the way! [58]

It was surely love at first sight;

    Therefore, he paid her price outright!

Sadly, soon after their love affair

    The unlucky maid catches cancer.

One carries a vase, looking hard for water.

    By the time he finds it, his vase may shatter.

One has a horse, scraping coins to buy a saddle.

    He gets the saddle, but wolves eat his whole cattle.

Medics were invoked one after another

    As two lives were in danger of one cancer!

The king, so frustrated and hopeless,

    Told them his love for her was endless;

Whoever could cure his honey,

    Would get lots of gifts and money.

They all promised the royal to do their best

    And join forces to lay her illness to rest.

They said they were each master of a domain;

    Therefore, they had medicine for every pain.

They didn't pray for God's will out of smugness,

---

[58] Every spirit (king) is on its way to uncover (hunt) the secrets of the universe and its origin; nonetheless, the spirit is always involved and distracted with the corporal obsessions (maid's sickness) of the human soul (maid).

So God wanted to prove human weakness! [59]

---

[59] The unsuccessful medics represent the philosophers and scientists who always try to resolve matters of humanity by applying just their material knowledge and overlooking God's providence or its spiritual interventions.

Not that praying strictly is of importance,

But the problem is neglecting God's presence.

One's soul may be in line with God's power

Without actually saying a prayer.

Even though the medics used all their guts and guile,

The girl's illness bizarrely went more volatile.

The girl became as thin as a hair,

So the king cried a river for her.

The medics' drugs had the wrong conclusion

Though they might've had the right solution!

Pouring water on fire is extinguishing

But it can, too, be very demolishing! [60]

Inability of Doctors and King Turning to God

Observing the doctors' lack of ability,

The king went to the mosque out of adversity.

After crying and saying some prayers,

He gave God the following words of praise:

"Oh, Lord! This world is your lowest kindness!

You surely know all that's inside one's breast.

Oh God! you always regard a wish.

I admit our flaws were too foolish.[61]

---

[60] When fire is out of electricity, pouring water on fire is more dangerous.

[61] The flaws committed by the medics and king as they didn't mind God during the medical treatment of the maid.

39

You did state: "Though I know your mysteries,

    I still want you to clearly ask your pleas."[62]

Since from deep down, he yelled out,

    The Lord's mercy dove flew out!

The king fell asleep while crying out;

    In his dream, an old man came about.

He said to the king: "your wish is granted;

    And soon someone would make you enchanted.

This man is an honest proficient medic;

    Observe the divine power in his magic!" [63]

King Greeting Visitor (New Doctor) [64]

The promising date was around the corner

    When the king saw a man by his tower.

Opening the door to enter the hallway

    He brought the light along, the whole way,[65]

---

[62] Apparently, Rumi's referring to these couple of quranic verses: Surah Al-A'raaf (7:55), and Surah Al-Ghafir (40:60) in which God asks the pious to clearly and hiddenly call his name and supplicate for their demands, and he will in return response.

[63] The new masterful doctor represents divine providence or a Sufi master by whom the king and the maid's (spirit and soul) problems and obsessions need to be cured.

[64] Transferred the Title: **Greeting of Visitor by King** to here where the interpreter believes it belongs for easier understanding of the reader. In the original this title comes after the title, **Importance and Benefits of Politeness, And Harms of Rudeness**.

[65] The new doctor brings along the godly light as if he was sent by God, denoting that he was sent from God with a divine mission (God's intervention).

نیست وَش باشد خیال اندر رَوان

Imagination may first appear unreal

تو جهانی بَر خیالی بین رَوان

But an imagination may run the whole deal

So he aroused the king's fascination

    Like an angel out of imagination!

Imagination may first appear unreal,

    But an imagination may run the whole deal!

Peace and warfare are placed on fantasy;

    Shame and honor are based on fantasy.

The fantasies, that are the saints' hooks,

    Are the paradise fairies' good looks.[66]

The fantasy that the king saw in his dream,

    Came out from the visitor's face like a beam.

The king then sprinted to meet his guest sent from above;

    Before his wardens, he greeted him with lots of love.

They have both sailed the divine love ocean

    And were tied without prior relation.

"My beloved is you not her," the king uttered

    "But then one thing leads to another in this world.

You're like Mohammad, and I'm your adherent;

    I'm all prepared to serve you like a servant!"

He asked about his journey and prominence

    And stated he found a treasure through patience.

---

[66] The fantasies that worked like a marketing hook to saints and mystics to keep them incited in spiritual path or to attract more Sufis and to the spiritual path, are the vision of cute fairies (representing any divine beauty in the universe) of heaven. In one of the stages of Sufism, Sufis or mystics will be able to intuitively vision the Lord's beauties in any creature or phenomenon of universe.

"You're the light of truth; you repel crisis.

You spelled patience as the key to solace.[67]

Seeing you is the answer to all queries.

Through you are easily solved all quandaries.

You translate whatever goes in a heart.

You back up whoever goes through a lot.

O God's chosen and favored one, welcome!

If you leave me, all grieves will again come.

You're the chief, and those, who reject that,

Will end up miserable and flat."

Pros and Cons of Politeness and Cons of Rudeness [68]

We ask God for good luck in politeness;

Since the rude are cut off from God's kindness.

The rude not only bring shame on themselves,

But also trouble all around themselves.

Food for the Moses tribe used to come from the skies

Without any efforts, discussions, sales, or buys!

Some of them rudely asked for more rice,

Then God fully stopped their food supplies.

They had to hardly farm for such a long interval,

Until Jesus pleaded with God for their survival.

Once more some of them rudely took their pots;

And went to Jesus again for more cuts.

---

[67] "Patience is the key to solace" is a quote by prophet Mohammad.

[68] By this section in the middle of the story, Rumi is trying to emphasize the importance of being polite and respectful to masters of spiritual knowledge, the same way that the king respected the divine doctor.

They tried to save food for another suspension;

    Jesus said: "this time there could be no cessation!"

But as cynical tactless thoughts are unrighteous,

    The holy universe stopped being generous!

The sky never rains from stingy clouds.

    No health ever comes from swinging clowns! [69]

In this world grief and darkness occurs

    When we're rude and selfish with affairs.

One who acts shamelessly on their way to Goddess,

    He's the wrong sign on others' paths and the meanest.[70]

Because of good manners, the sky is bright;

    Some souls are saints for their ethics are right.

King Taking New Doctor to See Maid

After some formality and salutation,

    It was time to start the examination.

---

[69] Swinging clowns represent people who demonstrate faithfulness in appearance to their relationship partner, but also swing between other sexual partners! Rumi, therefore, thinks having a relationship with someone who has multiple sexual partners is not healthy. In the next verse, Rumi as well implies that people who cheat sexually in their relationships are examples of rudeness and selfishness.

[70] Those who claim that they are taking the spiritual way but act shamelessly, cause others to get confused and distracted on their godly way and possibly lose the right direction. Hence, their behavior is unfair to others and they are the meanest people on earth.

He let the new doctor into his harem[71]

Since he was then a confidant with wisdom.[72]

He challenged the early prescription

That had worsened the situation.

They were unaware of the girls' inner mood,

So her real illness was misunderstood.

He figured out why the girl was suffering,

However, he didn't tell the king anything!

He realized from the way she whined

That her sickness was about her mind!

Her whine was a symptom issued from her heart!

Among the pains, the love pain is worlds apart!

No misery is the same as love miseries.

Love is a means of revealing God's mysteries.

Without considering which side love flows from,

At last, it'll lead us to that root it grows from! [73]

I keep describing love a lot; however,

Falling in love, I can't explain it whatsoever!

Though tongue may sound very descriptive;

Without it, love's more indicative.

---

[71] Harem, pronounced as /'hɛːrəm/, is the most inner part of a Muslim household dedicated to wives, and female servants, where stranger men are not allowed to enter.

[72] implying that a master of spiritual wisdom should be regarded as a confidant by seekers of the spiritual path, thus letting him enter their harem (world of secrets).

[73] In Rumi's idea, almighty God is the source of love and all types of love, whether earthly or celestial, eventually guide us to their genesis which is God itself.

NO MISERY

IS THE SAME AS

LOVE MISERIES

LOVE IS A MEANS OF

REVEALING

GOD'S MYSTERIES

علت عاشق ز علت‌ها جداست

عشق اصطرلاب اسرار خداست

The pen was writing all words smoothly fast,

But once it got to "love" it could not last!

Explaining it, the brain went into grief;

Just love could give us its own perfect brief.

The reason for both sun and shade is the Sun star.

Don't neglect the Sun if you need a rationale.[74]

The shade can be a clue to the Sun's existence,

But the Sun's bestowing life in every instance.[75]

Shade makes us sleep and dream just like a myth.

When the Sun rises, the dark ends forthwith.[76]

---

[74] Rumi here is comparing the apparent existence of love to the Sun by mentioning that although we can discover the being of the Sun through its effects like light and shade, we can as well directly prove the existence of the Sun by observing it directly (intuitionism). Therefore, as the Sun in the sky is the best reason for the actuality of itself (rather than shade or light), the divine love itself also is the best proof for being of it.

[75] Again, Rumi is insisting that the discovery of divine love needs no reasoning or rationality and can be only based on intuitionism (unveiling and intuition) because the same way that the Sun is proving its own existence by always being in the sky and granting warmth and comfort, divine love is likewise always granting energy of life to all species.

[76] Rumi is comparing human reasoning or wisdom to shade which despite being a clue to the existence of divine love (God), it can also cause neglect of the real source of love and warmth which resembles the Sun. However, when the Sun or love rises above all things, the strength of its light ends all darkness and shades and makes us needless of all neglecting reasonings and rationalities.

چون قلم اندر نوشتن می شتافت

The pen was writing all words smoothly fast

چون به عشق آمد قلم بر خود شتافت

But once it got to "love" it could not last

عقل در شرحش چو خر در گل بخفت

Explaining it, the brain went into grief

شرح عشق و عاشقی هم عشق گفت

Just love could give us its own perfect brief

The sun of spirit is also supernal;

It's alien but timeless and eternal.[77]

Though the sun out there is the solo one,

We can imagine one just like the Sun;

Yet the sun of spirit, enshrined and undefined,

Cannot be even imagined in any mind! [78] [79]

Request of New Doctor for Private Talk with Maid

The doctor went to ask the king,

To arrange a private meeting.

He wanted an isolated space,

So the girl could speak up in that place.

The doctor asked her about her race;

As a starting conversation case.

The girl slowly talked about every matter

---

[77] The spirit of humans resembles the Sun in the way that it is supernal and celestial, and looks as well far, familiar, and alien to us humans, but it's also eternal and timeless.

[78] The spirit of humans, which is enshrined (immortalized by God) and undefined, though resembling the Sun in its warmth-granting and celestiality, in contrast to the Sun, cannot be imagined and drawn in humans' minds.

[79] At the end of this section, Rumi composed multiple verses regarding his conversation with Hassan (one of his comrades mentioned in the preface of this book), in which Hassan requested Rumi to explain some legacies of the Shams who had an extraordinary effect on Rumi's mystic life. The word "Shams" in Persian means the Sun as well. That's why in the moment Rumi was composing these verses, Hassan gets reminded of Shams, asking Rumi to explain some of the Sufistic moments he shared with Shams. The interpreter has determined to skip these verses to help the reader stay more focused on the main story.

While her pulse was being checked by the master.

If a thorn gets into someone's skin,

Removal is tough as it's too thin.

Imagine a thorn goes into the heart;

Pulling it out will take a lot of art! [80]

If a thorn gets into a donkey's fetlock,

Just to make it worse, he kicks it to the rock!

As the girl was talking about her memories,

The doctor checked her symptoms amid her stories.

Nothing really proved to be out of hand

Until her story got to Samarkand!

She both blushed and paled, and her pulse quickened;

Once the talk reached a smith, her voice weakened.

As the doctor discovered her mystery,

He figured out the root of her misery.

He told her then he diagnosed her grief;

He would work miracles for her relief.

He warned: "tell no one about your mystery,

Though the king tries so hard for discovery."

When your affairs stay secret.

Your wish is earlier met.

A seed has to hide in the earth,

So that Later it can give birth.

The doctor's promising words and aid,

Eased the worries of the anxious maid.

---

[80] If someone gets heartbroken or his psych sickens, their treatment takes a lot of effort.

Real promises are pleasing.

Void pledges though are displeasing.

The nobles' promises are precious.

The ignobles' words are fictitious.

Diagnosis of Doctor and Expressing it to King

Then the doctor went to the king of glory

To acquaint him with a bit of the story,

Saying the plan was to invoke the smith;

The one who was the prince of the maid's myth!

The smith guy was required to be brought there

Even if it was by cash and cashmere!

Invocation of Smith by King

The king sent two envoys to smith's village

To present him with the great king's message:

"You've made a name as the best smith in society!

Therefore, you've been offered a role by our majesty.

The king has gifted you this cash and cashmere.

Should you take this role, you'll be his courtier."

Seeing that much bread and butter,

He opted to leave his counter.[81]

Not knowing of his real destiny,

He happily took on this new journey!

In life, we sometimes take an indulging path,

Not knowing of its terrible aftermath.

On his mind, he had the dream of power and wealth,

---

[81] Counter of his store.

51

But troubles could be waiting for his life and health!

چون که اسرارت نهان در دل شود

آن مرادت زودتر حاصل شود

When your affairs stay secret

Your wish is earlier met

As soon as he arrived at the king's castle,

    He was welcomed by his staff with no hassle.

The doctor took him to meet the king in homage.

    The king then showed him his copper and gold storage.

The king later was advised by the doctor

    To let the cute girl meet the smithing master

So that the girl could enjoy his affection,

    Eliminating her mood of affliction.

The love birds enjoyed each other's compassion,

    Getting the most out of the king's permission.

After six months of dalliance,

    The girl gained back her mood balance.

Then a syrup was made for the smith in stealth.

    His maid mixed it with his meals to spoil his health.

As he unknowingly kept eating this toxin,

    In the eyes of the girl, he got very weak and thin.

As the sickness ruined his attraction

    Moreover, he lost the girl's affection.

The romance following only an appearance

    Is not love but just a shameful experience!

I wish the look were also reprehensible,

    So that no misjudgment on it was possible.[82]

His nice eyes became the killer of his health!

    Now, bloody eyes overtook his looks and wealth!

---

[82] Rumi wishes that the look and appearance of shameful but attractive matters were also reprehensible, not only the final experience and reality behind it.

Peacock's ultimate foe is its feather

    Akin to a fox slain for its leather.

How many vain kings, who were valiant,

    Because of their pride, met their descent?

"I am like that elephant killed for its tusk",

    Said the smith to others before his last dusk,

"My killer should know, by God, he'll earn a sentence,

    For preferring a thing to a man's existence.

This world is a mountain, sound and round.

    We earn our deeds back like an echoed sound."

The poor smith then died in vain,

    So did the girl's love and pain

Since the love of mortals is evanescent

    And once they're gone, their senses are quiescent.

The alive love is fresher than a blossom

    At any second to our sight and wisdom.

Choose the love of an entity that's immortal,

    And its reviving love is timelessly vital.

Designate your love to that supreme entity

    From whom all saints got their holy identity.

Don't say God wouldn't love you since you're too sinful

    Because It's really far too merciful.

God Ordering Murder of Smith, not a Wicked Temper

The murder of the smith by the doctor

    Wasn't out of either a wish or horror,

Neither did he kill him for the king's greed;

    Goddess commanded his murder indeed.

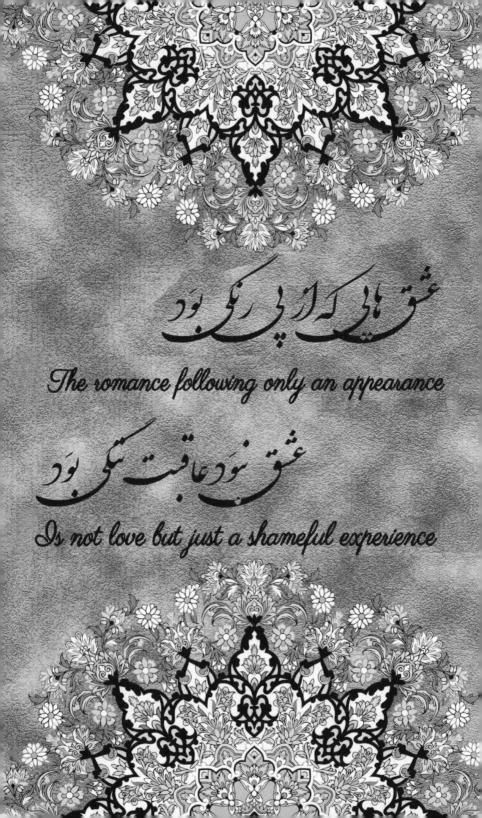

عشق هایی که از پی رنگی بود

The romance following only an appearance

عشق نبود عاقبت ننگی بود

Is not love but just a shameful experience

Even Moses couldn't guess when Khidr made that odd kill

That the victim would act later like an evil.[83]

If someone gets revelation from Goddess

Whatever they say is totally righteous.

The one who gifted us this body and soul

Can take them back through his means of prime control.

God's means, in this case, was the divine physician;

On earth, he was an agent of divine mission.

Surrender your head to God as Ishmael did,[84]

And sacrifice it happily like that kid

---

[83] Here Rumi is referring the reader to a quranic story (Surah Al-Kahf, 18: Verses 60-82) happening between Moses and Khidr. Khidr is supposedly one of God's chosen saints on the earth. According to Quran, Moses is introduced to Khidr to learn some divine lessons. Khidr accepts his company under the condition that Moses never questions Khidr's actions under any circumstances.

As the story unfolds, Khidr performs several bizarre actions; one being him killing a young man for no apparent reason. Moses questions this action and several other Khidr's actions and finally, Khidr unhappily leaves Moses telling him all the reasons for his odd behaviors: one being the reason for killing the young man as he will later rage against his parents who were God believers and cause them a lot of troubles but God later will give them a much better good-hearted kid.

[84] A referral to a quranic story (Surah As-Saffat, (37:104-105)) where Ibrahim is ordered by God in his dream to sacrifice his son Ismael. Although in the beginning, Ibrahim has some doubts, he eventually is determined to perform the sacrifice with the persuasion of Ismael. However, Ibrahim's knife loses its sharpness through God's providence, and a sheep is sent by God to him to be sacrificed instead of Ismael. Therefore, Ibrahim passes a major divine test successfully.

این جهان کوه است و فعل ما نِدا

سوی ما آید نداها را صدا

This world is a mountain sound and round

We earn our deeds back like an echoed sound

So that your soul stays forever joyous

    As it did for Mohammad's and Jesus'!

True lovers say cheers to get drunken

    When for love, their ego is sunken.

The king didn't kill the smith out of lust.

    Please don't think what he did was unjust.

We may assume that the king was very guilty,

    But no dirt may mess up an inborn purity!

As blistering heat melts away gold's excess,

    That harshness is to raise man's inner goodness.

The harsh experiments are like a hearth,

    Melting away the filth from people's hearts.

If God hadn't inspired the king's doing,

    He would've been a pig, not a king!

He was free of greed, temptation, and lust.

    What he did was right though seeming unjust.

Though Khidr's deeds seemed very wrong to Moses,

    His deeds totally had the right basis!

Even Moses, with all his divine knowledge,

    Could not understand Khidr's actions' message.

That move was rosy though seeming bloodstained.

    He's drunken with wit though looking insane!

The king was made special by the Holy Goddess.

    Anyone murdered by him will be glorious.

If God didn't see any good in the king's rage,

    Its divine mercy would not let that outrage.

Likewise, a mom doesn't stop her kid's injection,

In spite of seeing his tearful rejection.

God takes a bit, but then tons are granted

In a way that your mind gets enchanted.

Our perception is bound to our own surroundings.

Our judgment then is full of misunderstandings.

Commentary on King and Maid Story

While the story may sound a bit awkward in that the king took the smith's life without any justifiable reason, we have to realize that in Rumi's stories, the characters usually represent other general terms or entities which are related to more spiritual, psychological, or philosophical concepts.

The king in this story represents in general the human spirit which constantly tries hard to protect and nurture the human soul, which is represented by the maid. Like the king, the human spirit has tendencies to both spiritual and temporal worlds:

Once upon a time, there was a king of majesty,

Who was the head of both religion and sovereignty!

One day, he goes hunting on his horse

With his courtiers trailing on the course.

The king saw a cute maid on the way,

And lost his heart to her all the way!

Any spirit (king) is on its way to uncover (hunt) the secrets of the universe and its origin; nonetheless, the spirit is always involved and distracted by the corporal obsessions (maid's sickness) of the human soul (maid). In the eyes of Rumi and other Sufis, the spirit is the celestial essence of the human that exists exclusively for God and is timeless and eternal; however, the soul is the persona of human beings and is temporal but it has the capability to sense the spirit and its spiritual connection.

The unsuccessful medics represent the philosophers and scholars who always try to investigate in or resolve matters of humanity by applying just their material knowledge and overlooking spiritual interventions:

They didn't pray for God's will out of smugness

So God wanted to prove human's weakness!

عاشقان جامِ شرف را نوشكنند

كبر و دست و سرِ خويش و تنشان كنند

TRUE LOVERS SAY CHEERS TO GET DRUNKEN

WHEN FOR LOVE THEIR EGO IS SUNKEN

The spirit struggles to purify the soul (maid) from its ego and its materialistic secular desires (the smith). Therefore, even though the spirit (king) loves the soul (maid), through divine intervention (the good doctor), it lets the soul (maid) get drowned in her obsession with materialistic gains (smith) for a while.

As the story unfolds, though, the soul's (maid's) earthly enjoyments (smith) wear off, and she loses interest in them. Yet again, through divine providence (the good doctor), the soul finds its real source of comfort which is the human spirit (king) as the spirit is a higher component of human nature and exists exclusively for God.

In the following verse, Rumi is giving us a hint that the king in his story is actually something pure and godly in its nature, like the human spirit:

We may assume that the king was very guilty,

But no dirt may mess up an inborn purity!

Following the above verse, he also points out that this harshness, killing off all materialistic attachments (killing the smith) in this world, is necessary for the inner goodness and spiritual growth of humans.

As blistering heat melts away gold's excess,

That harshness is to raise man's inner goodness.

...

Surrender your head to God as Ishmael did

And sacrifice it happily like that kid

So that your soul stays forever joyous

As it did for Mohammad and Jesus!

In the above verses, Rumi, in fact, is advising everyone to happily sacrifice their ego (head) to get closer to God so that their soul becomes permanently joyous. Moreover, he comes up with this spiritual mystic key verse restating that to feel the true divine love, the God lovers have to sink their large ship of ego.

True lovers say cheers to get drunken

When for love, their ego is sunken.

Another important but implicit deduction, we can reach in this tale, is that human may really need some time to kill of his egoistic desires, and materialistic attachments to actually progress spiritually. We saw near the end of the story that the divine doctor advised the king to let maid and smith to freely bring on their romance till their zeal for each other wears off. However, divine providence and blessings do mysteriously intervene in human life from time to time to help the human to lose their zeal for materialistic possessions wear off and find their path towards spiritual development. This is encoded in Rumi's story by the divine doctor secretly feeding drug to the smith to gradually dismantle him.

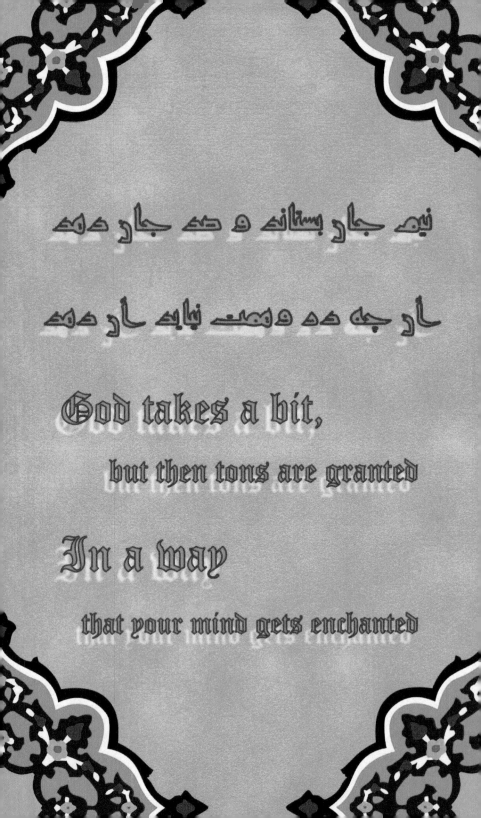

نیم جار بستانه و دد جار دمه

ارجه دد دمند نباید ار دمه

God takes a bit,

but then tons are granted

In a way

that your mind gets enchanted

Grocer and Parrot and Oil Spilling by Parrot

There was once a grocer with a pet

Which was a fluent talking parrot.

At the store, not only she was a keeper,

But she was also well known as a japer.

Once, flying and playing around the store

She broke bottles, spilling oil on the floor.

The grocer went back to open the store

Only to find all that oil on the floor.

Seeing his store floor so oily and wet,

He lost his temper and slapped the parrot.

The parrot went bald and mute for a while,

And the grocer rued what he did meanwhile,

Wishing God had broken his arm

>Before he broke his lucky charm[85].

He helped many broke ones get out of debt

>Just so that God brings back his tuneful pet.[86]

To get her talk, he used all likely schemes

>While sitting at the store with tears and screams.

One day, a bald dervish was passing by;

>At once, she decided to give him a hi.

She asked: "How come you got bald like a coot?

>Did you, too, spill oil somewhere on your route?"

The crowd there laughed so hard at her comparison

>As she applied her own story to that person.[87]

One shouldn't match the saints' deeds with their own.

>All are not hunters that blow the horn.

The reason for the whole world going astray

>Is that just a few understood the saints' way.

---

[85] Lucky charm is the parrot as his cuteness attracts customers into the Grocer's store.

[86] In Iranian culture, people make a vow to the Deity to take a compensating action, often of a charitable nature, in order for return of God's grace and blessing to them, or so that God actualizes what they asked him in their prayers. This culture is called "Nazr".

[87] In the following verses of this section, Rumi is criticizing misjudgment of humans based on analyzing all the events (even the ones not pertaining to them) by linking them to their own short knowledge and experience, and thereby, like a parrot, repeating the same reasoning and deducing the wrong causes from events and phenomena all over again.

Most think prophets and them are at the same rank,

 For, like all humans, they also ate and drank. [88]

However, out of bias and ignorance,

 They failed to grasp there is a huge difference.

Both bee types suck nectar on the same farm;

 One yields honey, the other causes harm! [89]

All canes taking water from the same rill,

 May not all end up in a sugar mill.

We would find lots of things looking similar,

 But in fact, their difference is way too far.

One snacked and became a case of obscenity.

 One other snacked to be the light of Deity.

Waters of spring and sea both look transparent,

 Although one tastes pleasant; the other pungent. [90]

---

[88] Rumi here is referring to couple of quranic verses: Surah Ibrahim, verse 10, (14:10); Surah Al-Furqan, verse 7, (25:7); Surah Al-Anbiya (the prophets), verse 21, (21:3) in which The Quran is narrating how people questioned the validity of God's prophets by reasoning that the prophets are just like other normal people.

[89] Historically in Iran (Persia), they apparently used to believe there are only two types of bees: one honeybee that yields honey and one wild bee whose sting can be harmful and fatal.

[90] In Rumi's analogy, the saints and virtuous people are like freshwater from springs as they are morally and spiritually pure and clean, and getting familiar with them makes your soul pure and fresh as well; however, the sinful people and pagans are like sea's saltwater as they are not morally pure and fresh, even though in surface they may look like good humans; hence friendship with them is a bitter and undesired experience. This analogy has been repeated various times throughout Masnavi.

Just connoisseurs have the authority on

    Distinguishing fresh water from salty one.[91]

Some equate prophets' miracles with magics,

    And believe they're both based on conjuring tricks.

Magicians, to oppose the word of God,

    Doggedly classed their wands with Moses's rod.[92]

Those wands are quite dissimilar to that stick.

    The contrast between those acts is gigantic.

One action was, in due course, cursed by God.

    The other was loyally blessed by God.

Pagans[93] are like monkeys in their debate.

    What others do, they'll blindly imitate.

To their soul, their lowly nature is a blight

    Causing them to not ever get their grounds right. [94]

---

[91] The other possible analogy is that Rumi may be resembling bad choices to saltwater and good choices in life to freshwater which are very hard to distinguish, thus we need a connoisseur to show us the right direction so that we don't taste or experience bad events or people in life.

[92] Rumi is pointing to the biblical/quranic story of Moses and pharaoh's magicians in which two sides compete over their supernatural capabilities. (Bible Exodus (7:11-22)) (Quran Yunus (10:75-83))

[93] "Pagan" is often used in this book to translate the word "Kafir" in Farsi meaning "non-believer". However, the more thorough translation would be "the people who try to conceal the truth". Therefore, whenever in this book you see the word "pagan" you should think of it as people who try to hide the truth.

[94] Rumi is blaming the deniers of prophets for blindly imitating and mocking their ancestors and each other (like a parrot) without deeply and thoroughly giving logical thought to the reason for the prophets' existence.

Apes think they're buying status by mocking humans,

    Yet they won't know the variance, nor will pagans.

Saints take steps based on God's glory and lenity;

    Pagans act based on their ego and enmity.

Hypocrites go to the mosque for rivalry.

    Their needs are not genuine but devilry.

If religious rites were like a baseball match,

    Hypocrites will lose it at last with no catch.

Though hypocrites and the frank play the same game,

    They're utterly too far from being the same.

Regardless, they each get what they deserve.

    They'll be ranked based on how frankly they serve.

Being called devout people, hypocrites get glad.

    Being called hypocrites, they become extra mad.

Devout people's name comes from their nice essence.

    Hypocrites' shame comes from their grim influence.

The word "devout" by itself has no quality.

    The word though describes an actual property.

If someone's labeled two-faced, he'll burn from the heart.

    Hence, wasn't, from the hell, this property set apart?!

It's not the term causing the shame of the label.

    A bowl cannot make its water undrinkable![95]

Each word's a bowl and the meaning, in it, water;

    The ocean of all meanings is the Creator.

---

[95] A word is just like a bowl that contains and describes an actual property, and that property can be pleasant or unpleasant like water.

The sea's saltwater never runs into rivers

    As if, in between, there are unseen barriers.[96] [97]

However, they both flowed out of one spring.

    Bypass them both and find that origin![98]

Pure gold and fake gold can't get separate

    Unless an expert assays their carat.[99]

Whoever is gifted with this shrewdness quality,

    They attain certainty in times of perplexity.

If a hair gets in an alive mouth,

    It won't relax until it is out!

---

[96] Quoted from Quran, Surah Ar-Rahman (The Most Beneficent), verses 19-20, (55:19-20).

[97] The same analogy is explained in footnote 90. Both groups (the virtuous/devout and the sinful/two-faced) may look similar to us in appearance (like freshwater and saltwater) and it may be hard to differentiate them, but they are still at variance in their nature.

[98] Sufis believe that all sorts of characters, whether good or bad, have been created by God. Rumi is inviting us to ignore the surface and attempt to discover the nature and origin of different characters; or else, it would be impossible to differentiate the two-faced from the truly devout.

[99] To be able to identify pure and devout characters from impure and two-faced ones, we need guidance from Sufi masters or senior mystics. They are like gold experts who can identify the impure gold from pure one.

If among all the food in the meal, a hair gets in;

Spotting it for a lively sense is an easy win.[100]

Earthly senses are the stairs to temporal success;

The moral sense, the stairs to mystical conquest!

For the health of earthly senses, ask a doctor.

For the fitness of moral sense, ask a master.

For the former, the body shall gain attention.

For the latter, the body shall face desertion!

The mystic way deserts the fleshly demands,

But then it enriches the souls of humans!

Some ruin their house to dig out precious metals,

So that instead, they can later construct castles.

Even so, no one can make rules for God's ways.

Yet what I just said was needed anyways.

How God does things might even seem discrepant.

The spiritual way is full of puzzlement.

Not puzzled as in not paying God attention,

But as in being adrift in the love ocean.

---

[100] The distinction between truth and falsehood, and between purity and hypocrisy is very difficult in this world as they all present themselves constantly in our lives, and this would leave us with so many unwanted doubts. So, Rumi is analogizing the doubts to hairs that occasionally may enter our mouth (life or brain). Luckily, we have been given the gift by God, inside us, to spot facts among doubts, and truth from falsehoods. However, to do so, we need to clean ourselves from sins and worldly attachments so that we purify our lively sense, and our intuition can correctly distinguish the good from the bad.

One faces God as a fact always prime;

    One's face reminds us of God all the time![101]

Observing both groups closely makes an impact

    So that you, too, always uncover the fact.

Any day, we may see a two-faced snake,

    So we shouldn't naively trust their handshake!

Hunters fake a tweet sound to lure birds in the air.

    Hearing the sound of their own, they land on a snare!

The ignoble steals Sufis' statements

    To deceive poor naive innocents.

The great men's manner is warmth and transparency;

    The cheap men's way is deceit and indecency.

They wear Sufis' woolen[102] to make a cheap cent;

    They then baptize a phony "a Living Saint"!

Mohammad's name through the time stayed sacred.

    What is left of his foes is just hatred.

---

[101] The first couplet is talking about a person who simply accepted God as a prime fact in the universe which is a major step in spirituality; an example of this person can be a Sufi newbie. The second couplet refers to a master Sufi, or a senior mystic, or a saint in a way that when others see him and meet him, they get reminded of God.

[102] As mentioned in footnote 17, Sufis were given a run-down woolen robe by their master to wear as a recognition of their sincerity and devotion and likewise as a sign to their spiritual non-materialistic life.

آنـکی یـک رادی او شدی سـوی دوسـت

و آنـکی یـک رادی او خـودروی دوسـت

One faces GOD

as a fact always prime

One's face reminds us of

GOD all the time

The wine[103] of truth refreshes the lover.

Cheap wine leaves just a stinky hangover.[104]

Deciphering the Story of Grocer and Parrot

The first character mentioned in this tale is the grocer. The grocer is actually a representative of people who are opportunistic and materialistic for the most part, and they only perform their religious duties to gain temporal benefit rather than the spiritual knowledge of universe. Remember that the grocer lost his temper so severely over few broken bottles of oil without even seeking for the reason of the incident, and that he even hurt his parrot who was practically present at his store to attract more customers. Then he again becomes overly dramatic over his parrot's muteness and baldness, and start helping others financially in hope for return of God's favor so that he keeps making money with his lucky charm or parrot.

Seeing his store floor so oily and wet,
    He lost his temper and slapped the parrot.
The parrot went bald and mute for a while,
    And the grocer rued what he did meanwhile,
Wishing God had broken his arm
    Before he broke his lucky charm.
He helped many broke ones get out of debt
    Just so that God brings back his tuneful pet.
To get her talk, he used all likely schemes
    While sitting at the store with tears and screams.

We have to note that the attractive colorful feathers of parrot are a symbol of earthly belongings, and when the grocer notice parrot's baldness, he gets

---

[103] In Sufism's terminology, wine represents the divine truth, and realizing the truth in this world is so bracing as if you're drinking a glass of fine wine.

[104] It seems that in this context, the wine of truth represents the saints and mystics as they can represent us the truth and spirituality of life, not just the truth of life and existence. In contrast, the cheap wine represents the two-faced and hypocrites who cause damage to spirituality which is the ultimate goal of religions.

so upset as his parrot has no attraction any longer to drive customers in the store.

Rumi used the parrot character to represent the people who blindly imitate others' actions or instructions and keep repeating them without giving them a deep thorough thought because parrots likewise mimic human speech and words and keep repeating them without really thinking about them.

Moreover, this kind of people also have the bad habit of judging others superficially based on their own deficient knowledge and experience. The reason for this behavior of theirs is that since they always blindly repeat other's behaviors or make judgements without deeply looking into matters and really attaining a thorough knowledge about them.

She asked: "How come you got bald like a coot?

Did you, too, spill oil somewhere on your route?"

The crowd there laughed so hard at her comparison

As she applied her own story to that person.

The parrot doesn't realize that the dervish has intentionally shaved his hair as a symbol of putting aside the earthly belongings and to avoid relations with materialistic superficial people, thereby adding to his spirituality knowledge in seclusion far from the clamors and turmoil of the world by worship and meditation.

Rumi further criticizes this kind of deficiency in people, and emphasizes that this obscene trait is one of the main characteristics of pagans (people who try to hide or deny the truth in general).

Pagans are like monkeys in their nature.

What others do, they'll blindly ape later.

To their soul, their lowly nature is a blight

Causing them to not ever get their grounds right.

Apes think they're buying status by mocking humans,

Yet they won't know the variance, nor will pagans.

Rumi warns as well that there are many greedy frauds around us who can easily take advantage of us through this superficiality deficiency of humans

At anytime, we may meet a two-faced fraud,

So we shouldn't just welcome everyone on board!

In the end, Rumi believes that the wisdom and knowledge of humankind is very limited even if they acquire vast knowledge and experience, so when they step in the path of spiritual discovery of universe, they still get empuzzled.

Even so, no one can make rules for God's ways.

Still, what I just said was needed anyways.

How God does things might even seem discrepant.

The spiritual way is filled with puzzlement.

جود بس اابير اه ه ه ده ه سد

بر به م دمز نشاب ه ه ه ه حسد

At anytime

we may meet a two-faced fraud

So we shouldn't just welcome everyone

on board

Jew King Killing Christians out of Bigotry

After the rise of christ, there ruled a Jew

Who oppressed the Christians without a clue.

Jesus' and Moses' seemed different

To this mislead cross-eyed tyrant.[105]

A master asked his cross-eyed beginner,

Once, to bring a glass from a container.

The beginner said: "There are two,

So which one should I bring to you?"

---

[105] This poem is a metaphor for any situation where a religious leader or a ruler of a theocratic state persecutes another group of people who follow a different belief system. The poem shows that the persecutor is ignorant and blind to the truth that all religions are connected and share the same source. The poem invites us to look beyond the superficial differences and see the common essence of all faiths.

Spiritual Rhymes (On Recognition of Soul & Ego)

The master said "That's just not true.

You're a squint. You see one as two!"

"Master! It's not nice to taunt one other."

    He said then: "Drop one of the glasses there!"

Once he dropped the glasses, they were all gone.

    Since it seemed two to him, but there was one!

Human gets cross-eyed due to lust and bigotry;

    Psych loses balance after spleen and zealotry.[106]

When selfish aims overcome, virtue gets disguised.

    Countless shields fill the gap between the heart and eyes.

If judges give in to hush money,

    How can they overcome villainy? [107]

That king, out of his Jewish partiality,

    Killed many believers of Christianity.

Minister Teaching shenanigans to King

The king hired a pagan minister full of tricks

    To achieve the impossible with politics.

He directed on stoppage of killing Christians

    As they would hide their rites to save their existence.

"Thousands of masks conceal their inner purpose;

    Their face is pro you, but their heart is factious!"

The king asked then what should be for them the scheme

    So that none of them survive, hidden or seen.

---

[106] Rumi explains how prejudice, fanaticism, and lust blind our third eye, spirit's eye or intuition, and causes the spirit to lose its straightness in the path of spiritual perfection and to get misguided.

[107] Rumi is giving examples how spite, self-interest and corruption can fog the power of human judgment in identifying the truth, and the beauty of arts and virtues.

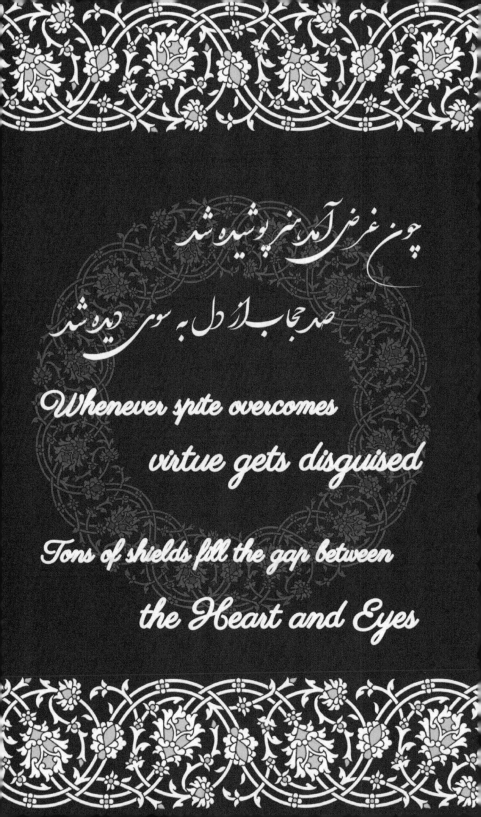

چون غرضی آمد هنر پوشیده شد

صد حجاب از دل به سوی دیده شد

Whenever spite overcomes

virtue gets disguised

Tons of shields fill the gap between

the Heart and Eyes

"You should convict me in the court of the city

    To the death penalty for some atrocity.

The hanging should happen in a crowded street,

    But to halt the drop, a peer should intercede.

To make it more credible, cut off my nose and ear,

    And burn all my properties in a tremendous fire.

Then send me far away to their settlement,

    So I sneak into their crowd to cause torment."

Minister Impersonating as a Christian

"I'll pose as a believer of the Bible

    Who's been concealing his faith for survival;

Yet you at last figure out my real religion,

    And you sentence me to the rope of execution.

I'll tell them: "On the king, my words lost their effect;

    My moods triggered the notions in his intellect.

My moods were like a peephole via which

    He read my mind without trusting my speech."

I'll tell them: "If it wasn't for Jesus' help, I'd be dead;

    I love his book, and for it, I'd sacrifice my head,

But it'll be sad if the holy faith of Christians

    Falls into pieces by the king's Jewish missions.

I'm sick of personating a Jew for the king.

    It's Jesus' time, and let all folks know it's his spring.""

The king did it all exactly as he told,

Baffling the people waiting by the scaffold.[108]

He exiled him to the Christians' land,

To land the final phase of what was planned.

Christians Falling for Minister's Deceit

He started holding sessions on Christianity.

Gradually thousands joined him from their community.

He was a holy apostle outwardly

Although a phony imposter inwardly.

That is why The Messenger's[109] companions

Asked about the sly ego's deceptions[110]

That what signs of veiled intents it can blurt out

While pretending to be sincerely devout.

They weren't too concerned with the merits of decencies;

They were seeking invisible deficiencies.[111]

They learned to pick out the cunning ego's tricks

Slowly but surely, using his hints and tips.

Even His hair-splitting comrades would marvel

Over His majestic pieces of counsel.

---

[108] The scaffold of the execution.

[109] The Messenger is one of the nicknames of the Prophet Muhammad.

[110] The deceiving ego is like a deceiving person as they both persuade the soul into committing unjust, awry and selfish actions and thus entrapping the soul into its egoistic state and not letting it elevate to its higher state.

[111] Mohammad's disciples were concerned rather with flaws and deficiencies of supposedly devout manners, that a deceiving soul or ego may blurt out to them, than just the merits of devout manners.

Christians Following Minister

Idolized by Christians, he earned lots of respect.

Who can deny the supporting masses' effect?![112]

He was regarded as a holy priest,

But in fact, he was a bloodthirsty beast.

Oh, Lord! Lots of baits and traps are in this world,

And we're each like a greedy and needy bird.[113]

Even if we each turned into a phoenix,

The traps of life would enhance their theatrics![114]

Oh, God! Although you rescue us every time,

We walk again towards another scourge slime!

---

[112] Rumi warns about the possible negative effects of masses supporting wrong idea or an illegitimate figure as they can cause a whole nation go astray.

[113] Baits and traps are the symbols of any corporal and temporal incentives that drive human lust, temper, and greed.

[114] Even if after a while humans think they are now strong, experienced and well-equipped against the baits and traps of life, the world starts laying down newer and harder traps for them. Therefore, the human has to be always very careful and considerate to not fall for tricks of its egoistic or egotistic desires when facing these new traps and learn to stay safely in their godly path. For one thing, the human may perform spiritual deeds for show-off to people, even if there is just a bit of intent for show-off, and not for real love and happiness of the Deity, that will reduce the integrity and credit of its actions.

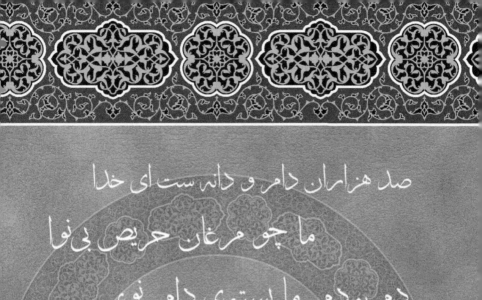

صد هزاران دام و دانه‌ست ای خدا

ما چو مرغان حریص بی‌نوا

دم‌به‌دم ما بستهٔ دام نویم

هر یکی گر باز و سیمرغی شویم

Oh, Lord!

Lots of baits and traps are in this world

And we're each like a greedy and needy bird

Even if we each turned into a phoenix

The traps of life would enhance their theatrics!

We hardly store wheat in a warehouse;

    Later we lose it all to a mouse;[115]

Nevertheless, we don't pay close attention

    That this loss is due to the mouse deception.

The mouse has dug a hole into our storage,

    Stealing our reserves, and causing us damage,

So dear! Please first get rid of this mouse;

    Then retry to save in your warehouse.[116]

Muhammad said once that no prayer is whole

    Unless with the sincere presence of the soul.

If there is no mouse stealing our wheats,

    Then where is the product of our deeds? [117]

So why doesn't our daily grace

    Add up to our storage place?

Nice deeds are like flying sparks,

    Slowly lighting the soul's darks;

---

[115] "Wheat" represents human deeds, warehouse or storage represents human soul, and mouse symbolizes very subtle egoistic deceptions that penetrate the purity and integrity of the human soul. Mystic newbies or generally people try hard to perform valuable deeds to add value to their credit and integrity, and thereby elevate the purity and worth of their soul (warehouse). However, their soul gets easily deceived by their ego (mouse), thereby losing all the spiritual integrity they have gathered.

[116] Rumi here asks us first to let go of all egoistic deceptions and then start committing good deeds with pure sincerity, i.e., not for show-off, duplicity, two-facedness, and popularity amongst people.

[117] If our souls have really not been stolen or deceived by the mouse of ego, where is the honest effect of spirituality in our soul and personality?

Yet, a hidden thief out of the dimness

Attempts to take out the soul's vividness.

If there are lots of lures to distort our path,

There's no worry if you, Lord, support our path.

Each night you free our soul from its fleshly cage;

They get free of all constraints, judgments, and rage. [118]

Sleeping, kings aren't aware of their empowerment,

And convicts are clueless about their confinement;

There's no concern for loss and interest;

There's no thought of this and that and the rest![119]

A mystic's state, though, can be like that without sleep;

He's numb to this world as in godly thoughts, he's deep.[120]

To a mystic, this world's pointless and worthless;

He is like a pen in the hand of Goddess.[121]

---

[118] Rumi believes that God invokes all the spirits while their flesh is sleeping.

[119] At night, when sleeping, all people are away from their daily and worldly matters.

[120] Mystics or Sufi masters are so much deep in their celestial and divine thoughts as if they are numb and inattentive to this world's matters, i.e., they are analogically asleep in this world as they have closed their eyes to temporal commotions and attractions. Likewise, Rumi possibly is declaring here that a highly Spiritual Mystic's soul or spirit can elevate towards the heavens even without sleeping.

[121] As this world and its matters are unimportant to mystics, they are always convinced with what God's intervention imposes on their lives and they are, therefore, like a pen in God's hands.

A cartoon, unable to see the hand,

    Thinks the pen tip gives the drawing command![122]

To reveal a bit of that gnostic condition,

    Slumber robbed the spirit of all men and women.[123]

In sleep, souls travel to a matchless savannah,

    And they pacify both their spirit and soma;

Next, God invokes all souls back to their skeletons,

    So they take on their daily duties and burdens.

The soul's horse loses its saddle again at night;

    "Sleep's the brother of death" by Ahmad[124] was so right!

On the horse limb, though, God fastens a chain,

    So that, daytime, it returns from that plain.

I wish you saved me like Noah against the sea wave,

    Or kept my flesh like the seven sleepers'[125] in a cave

---

[122] Now here Rumi is emphasizing that indeed everything and every event in this world happens through God's providence; however, most people fail to understand this as they are limited to physical constraints this world imposes on them; the same way that a cartoon, drawn on a paper will never be able to see anything outside of that paper, so he can't percept that there is actually a hand behind the moving pen tip that is drawing the other cartoons on the paper.

[123] To illustrate a bit of mystics' spiritual state to people, God created sleep for them because, as Rumi believes, during sleep, souls or spirits get disconnected from their bodies.

[124] Another title for Prophet Mohammad

[125] The Seven Sleepers, or Companions of the Cave, is a medieval legend narrated in Quran and Bible, which is about a group of youths hiding inside a cave around 250 A.D. to evade Roman persecutions of Christians. They miraculously fell asleep in their hideout and they woke up 300 years later.

So that I could shield my spirit's awareness

Against the storm of this dreadful wakefulness.[126]

There may be some sleepers around us this instant,

But what's the use when we aren't amply observant.[127]

The Caliph Meeting Lailey

Caliph said to Layla: "Is it you really

The cause of Majnoon's distress and Insanity[128]

For, compared to other beauties, you're not that pretty?!"

She replied: "Hush, since you've never been a devotee!"

Those who are awake are truly asleep

When their alertness is worse than their sleep;

---

[126] Rumi wishes, even while being awake, he could keep enjoying this protection by God that Sufis take advantage of when they lose their earthly consciousness and their soul/spirit travel to the spiritual/semantic world. Therefore, he wishes that he was asleep in the cave like the seven sleepers, and his soul was with God's protection while his body was asleep in a cave, or that his soul was protected like Noah's against the waves and storms of his awake ego.

[127] At every moment in a time around us there are mystic people like the seven sleepers who can guide us spiritually and share their knowledge with us; however, as we are too busy with our lives and we cannot identify and get to know these mystics truly.

[128] Rumi is referring to a famous Iranian (Persian) love story, called *Layla and Majnun* (pronounced like "Majnoon") composed by the Iranian poet *Nizami Ganjavi*, in which Majnun's love for Layla is very decent and pure, but not everybody understands the reason of Majnun's crazy love for Layla, as Layla was really not that beautiful in appearance. Moreover, "Majnun" is actually the nickname people name him by as it literally means "insane" in Farsi and he was insanely in love in their eyes.

If our soul isn't awake to the Deity,

    This alertness is only captivity![129]

So immersed with thoughts of loss and benefit,

    And always facing the fear of deficit,

Our soul is left with neither sincerity

    Nor glory nor a path to the Deity.

Those who make a wish of every dream out of hand,

    And get too swayed by it, are, in fact, in dreamland.

In their dreams, they consider a devil a sprite,

    Hence, they sleep with her out of lustful appetite!

Once, unfruitfully, they release their semen,

    The dream escapes, and they get reawakened,

Left with only some dirt and mental grief.

    Aw, what a fictional transient belief![130]

---

[129] If we aren't aware of spiritual world and are just concerned with the corporal world, our soul isn't really awake even if it's physically awake, this kind o alertness is useless or can be even harmful (meaning of the last two verses).

[130] In the last four verses, Rumi is criticizing the greedy materialistic people who get too excited about every temporal attraction and start dreaming and fantasizing about it constantly. Moreover, they keep spending too much time and effort to accomplish a dream that will neither satisfy them enough nor rectify their spiritual needs. Therefore, after the dreams are gone, they don't feel gratified and realize that their lifetime, youth, and energy (represented by semen) was wasted on too many empty dreams that didn't even play a supportive role in their souls' happiness. So, they still remain in disturbance, confusion, and uncertainty causing them mental grief, and they regret how fleeting and unreal their dreams and beliefs were.

The bird's in the sky, flying around,

  While its shade is moving on the ground;

Then a fool starts chasing the shadow

  Until its energy gets all low,

Not knowing whose shade that portrayal is,

  Not knowing where the original is!

He would keep chasing and shooting the shade

  Until his life bullets completely fade. [131]

As long as the divine shade becomes our nurse,

  It'll look after us through shadows and desires.

The divine shade is merely a Goddess' servant,

  He's temporally dead but mystically sentient.

Wo should resort to their laps with no doubt,

  The laps you won't survive doomsday without.[132]

---

[131] Rumi is metaphorizing the truth of God's intervention in all matters, to a bird flying all around the earth so that everything else is just a shade portrayed by God's light. However, most people fail to realize that there is a source of light and love that gets imaged by all other beings in the world, so they just keep chasing the materials for wealth and power, neglecting that they can be spiritually and meaningfully powerful by just connecting themself to that almighty origin of power, thus completely wasting their life energy on invaluable matters (meaning of last 4 verses).

[132] Rumi again recommends us to consult with a mystic or Sufi master or anyone who possesses divine spiritual knowledge to learn how to manage our life amid all these worldly attractions and distractions, since the possessor of divine knowledge is not too dependant or excited about attractions of this world, and he mostly cares to act vibrantly in accordance to god's will and pleasure, as if he is dead for this world and alive only for God's purposes.

جان همه روز از لگدکوب خیال

وز زیان و سود وز خوف زوال

نی صفا می ماندش نی لطف و فر

نی به سوی آسمان راه سفر

So immersed with thoughts of loss and benefit

And always facing the fear of deficit

Our soul is left with neither sincerity

Nor glory nor a path to the Deity

Extending God's shade is the role of saints

As they're the reason for Its[133] glow's presence.

We should not step on this path without these reasons;

Like Abram, let's not bow before ephemerons.[134]

If envy takes over us on the way,

The devil will certainly hold our sway.

As out of envy, he scorns humanity,

And defies its eternal felicity.[135]

Lucky are those who're quite empty of jealousy;

No snag is more impassable on this journey.

If this body hosts enviousness,

It will taint our intuitiveness.

Although this flesh is earthly and may host envy,

It can, too, be a source of light and purity.

If one envies those free of enviousness,

Darkness will cloud over the shine of their breast.

---

[133] Using "Its" to refer to what's God's.

[134] The same way that shadow is a reason for the existence of light, a saint or mystic is as well a reason for the presence of God, thus saints are like an extension of God's shade and shelter that will protect us by guiding us to the right path, and we need them to avoid dropping our fate into laps of idols that fade and perish. The last couplet points to a quranic verse, in Surah Al-An'am (6:76), in which it quotes a saying of Abram (Abraham), the prophet, in which he declares to people who worship Sun and Moon that he wouldn't worship a god that wanes or goes down.

[135] Rumi is warning us to beware of our possible envy to saints and mystics on our way to spiritual improvement because it can put our sway in hands of the devil or our deceptive ego and will obstruct our mystical development since the devil is the enemy of humanity and puts all his efforts to prevent their eternal rapture.

We should be humble around men of verity

And bury our envy and insecurity.

Explaining Jealousy of the Minister

The minister's essence was filled with envy,

So he had his ear and nose cut off vainly.

He pinned his hopes on inflaming the Christians

With the fire of his envy and malignance.

Those who, out of envy, stick their nose in the air

Have indeed left themselves with no nose, eye, and ear.

Deprived of a nose, how could he follow his nose?

To have a nose for the truth, he needed this nose!

One who can't smell the scent of truth is noseless.

That scent's heavenly and is sourced from Goddess.[136]

If one scented the truth and didn't cherish it,

Ingratitude would cause their insights to quit.

One should praise the grateful saints and be their servant.

By complying with them, the soul stays resilient.

We shouldn't distance people from their Deity,

And get by through misleading humanity.

The rogue minister became one of those parsons

Who equivocates to delude other persons

---

[136] In the last three verses, Rumi indicates that if a person due to jealousy gets so arrogant about their thoughts and beliefs (like the minister) and acts on it, that jealousy will blind his senses and intuition (represented by "nose"), and he(she) will lose his ability to trace the divine source of all lovely matters and concepts in this world.

94

Clever Ones Figuring out Duplicity of Minister

In his speech, the passionate sensed harmony,
  But the smart ones also saw acrimony.
He gave them lots of tips mixed with intentions
  As if he poured them honey mixed with poisons.
His public facade cheered sharpness in piety,
  But in effect, it guided them to laxity.
Although the fire, at first, looked nicely scarlet,
  In action, it blackened everything it met.
For those whose insight was not that perfect,
  His hints were like a curse around the neck.
The sly minister went through six years of exile,
  Gaining the trust of most Christians using his guile.
The people confided in him on divine topics,
  And they would aspire to his directions and edicts.

Hidden Communication of King and Minister

The king wrote to him to see if they were still on track.
  He assured him all was set for the final attack.
He asked the king to let him keep the progress
  For he was near to crush what's left of Jesus.

Explaining Twelve Tribes of Christians

There were twelve primates for the Christians;
  Each would lead a tribe of adherents.
The twelve tribes were all troubled by the vile minister.
  They all obeyed the words and acts of this fake pastor.
Their primates even obeyed his deeds
  Since they were blindly obsessed with his creeds.

95

Minister Mixing Bible Commandments Vigorously

For each tribe, he wrote a scroll of commandments

While each one included different contents.

In one scroll, he outlined fasting and penance

As a must for acceptance of repentance;

In one other, he rejected fasting and penance,

Saying charity is the only deliverance.

In another, he counted fasting and charity

As cases of idolatry and impiety!

In short, each scroll had something against the other.

How can honey and garlic taste like each other?

Until we don't overlook this diversity,

How can we enjoy the gardens of unity?[137]

Thereby devising twelve different creeds,

That Jesus' foe divided Jesus' breeds.

Practices Causing Religion's Breaches, not their Truth

The minister wasn't aware of Jesus' plainness.

Jesus' vat had only one color of frankness.

---

[137] Rumi, emphasizes that the discrepancies between the minister's scrolls were so obvious to common intelligence. It seems like, here, Rumi is trying to explain or even criticize the apparent differences among religions. Though he believes in their outward differences (represented by the difference of garlic and honey), he also believes in the unity of their foundations, and he encourages us to accept and pass over this diversity to enjoy the lavishness of unity of all humans.

Jesus dyed all those colorful clothes one hue.

He showed all his true colors, being true-blue![138]

This plainness isn't of the type causing stagnation

But of that clarity, fish love in the ocean.

Though on the land, the varieties abound,

The fish hate the colorfulness of the ground.[139]

What are ocean and fish in this comparison

So that they echo God's greatness within reason?!

Tons and tons of oceans and fish, in their essence,

Bow low to revere Its bounty and eminence.

---

[138] Rumi is referring to a biblical story within the apocryphal Syriac Infancy Gospel, in which young Jesus was working for a dyer named Salem. One day, Salem decides to go on a trip, thereby giving Jesus a bunch of cloth to dye different colors while he is out of town. However, when he returns, he gets furious at Jesus for he realizes that Jesus has thrown all clothes in the indigo vat. Eventually, Jesus takes them out one by one in the right colors using his magic.

Rumi is using this story analogically to demonstrate that the faith (color) of the Lord is only one color and that's the religion of plainness, frankness and faithfulness (like the color of Jesus). However, different prophets or generally different people with faith may have various ways of expressing it or different takes or perceptions of it, resulting into all these different religions (the different dyes of clothes that eventually come out of Jesus' vat) we see in today's world. Nevertheless, the essence of all religions is the same as they all come from the same origin (represented by Jesus' indigo Vat).

[139] Jesus' plainness doesn't create boredom and stagnation, but it is the consistent and transparent source of love like the ocean. That's why the fish love the ocean with all its uniformity and transparency and resist leaving it for the land with all its varieties and colorfulness. The same way Sufis, realizing the depth of divine love ocean, will never leave it for the earthly colorful attractions.

How much mercy has rained on oceans

    Such that pearls glorify their basements?! [140]

God has shed glare of science on water and earth

    So that they nurture seeds till their life-giving birth.

In this loyal earth, you reap what you sow.

    It returns you what you seed with no blow.

This trust from God[141] could earn its trustability

    From the brightness shined by the sun of equity.

Until the spring doesn't stage the sign of Creator,

    The earth won't manifest the secrets of nature.[142]

That Goddess, who gave the lifeless

    These trusts, specifics, and rightness,

---

[140] Please refer to footnote 41 for explanation of ancient belief of Iranians on how a pearl is created.

[141] Rumi thinks of earth and soil as a trust given by the Lord

[142] In the last 14 couplets, Rumi is specifying that all creatures have a certain function (like the one of the earth's), and their functions are constantly ordered and coordinated by the Almighty God, like the appearance of spring only after God allows the plants to regrow or reawake from their hibernation. Therefore, in a way all things in the universe abide by some kind of uniformity enhanced by the lord as if they are all part of one intelligent and homogeneous system.

Through Its grace, can make the inanimate conscious

While through Its scorn, makes the intelligent senseless.[143]

My heart can barely sustain this passion;

Who shall I tell? No ear's there to listen!

Yet where there was an ear, it turned to vision;

Stones may turn into gems through Its benison.

This praise of mine, though, is as bad as quitting praise;

It means I singly exist, and this being's off base! [144]

We have to feel hollow before Goddess' presence,

Besides flaws and grieves, what else is our existence?

For one thing, if our senses were flawless,

How come we haven't yet sensed God's warmness?

---

[143] Mystics, and Sufis, through studying quranic verses and prophet's quotes, and through their intuition, realized that all beings, whether inanimate or animate, are equipped with some sort of consciousness, and all beings in nature abide by certain rules set by God, and they can perform their God given duties with the help of specifics that the Lord has given them. Nevertheless, some of the intelligent people choose to deny the existence of God and defy his orders, thus God scorns their presence and they deprive themselves of Its unified system of mercy and favor, and subsequently, they become like senseless and unconscious objects in the system of the universe.

[144] Sufis believe the final stage of spiritual perfection is to dissolve their spirit into God as if their existence and God's forms one union of spirit, i.e., their soul doesn't singly exist, thus God and godly matters will be their only concern. In this verse, Rumi as well emphasizes the necessity of unification with God by stating that even praise and worship to God may mean that the worshiper and God are separate entities and that may defy the Sufis' understanding of unity. This statement though does have a bit of exaggeration (very common in Iranian poems) to enlighten the signification of unity to the reader.

If we were not laden with grief and debacle,

    When would this world be frozen like an icicle? [145]

Loss of Minister in his Deceit

Just like the king, the minister was superficial,

    As he picked a battle with a timeless essential [146]

Who can create an untold universe

    In a flash from absolute nothingness!

Many worlds will be uncovered to your sight

    If the Deity enlightens your insight.

This world may seem immense and infinite,

    But beside God's might, it's only a whit.

Beware that this world is a cage for our spirits,

    Yet they can thrive to reach the plains of no limits.

This world's finite, but the spirit's perennial;

    To that, face and form are blocking material.[147]

God smashed all the pharaoh's spears with one Moses' rod;

    So many doctors fell poor against Jesus' lifeblood;

---

[145] Rumi believes if we were all spiritually smarter to feel every minute of divine presence in our world and lives, the world would be a better place to live and it would not be so frozen and depressed like an ice.

[146] The almighty God is meant here as passage of time has no effect on It and It is essential part of our lives and the universe no matter what.

[147] Our face and body in this world act as a temporary blockage to our eternal and infinite spirit which has a tendency to go back to its infinite cosmos where it belongs. However, even in this world, our spirit has the capability to spiritually flourish infinitely and sense the divine truth.

So many books by philosophers were written,

But none could've words of an unschooled man[148] beaten.[149]

Who can not admire a triumphal God like that

Unless one who's a lowly despicable gnat?!

God had many artful foxes outwitted,

And had many stony hearts inspirited.

Endowing minds with guile isn't of this venture;[150]

Only the broken face Its graceful feature. [151]

How many wheeler-dealers did that snake toy?!

What's a snake anyhow to be its fake toy?![152]

---

[148] Referring to Prophet Muhammad as he was unlettered when The Quran was revealed to him.

[149] An intelligent contrast is done by Rumi in the last two verses when he is comparing the limited and deficient power and wisdom of humanity against the Lord's. The last verse is comparing the influence of the Quran with other textbooks.

[150] The venture of spirituality.

[151] Only those whose egos are broken will benefit from God's grace and fervor, not those who are constantly to improve their wile and guile to earn more temporal power.

[152] Wheeler-dealers represent those so-called Christian sages who were fooled by the crafty minister(snake).

When a woman was red-faced of her vileness,

   Holy Lord remoulded her into Venus.[153]

A skirt[154] conversion to rock is regression,

   But becoming a toy isn't degradation?

Our spirit could raise us all the way to the skies,

   But we've lowered our soul to the level of flies!

---

[153] Rumi is drawing on a myth about two supposedly fallen angels, Harut and Marut, in which they both insist that God send them to the earth to enjoy living there as they believe humans don't know how to enjoy blessings of living on the earth and to thank and worship God at the same time. Therefore, God agrees with their request but after remoulding them to a human, thereby giving them human lust and nature.

At a point in their earthly life, they both meet the same beautiful woman separately, and they both ask her to sleep with them. The woman though tells them that it's prohibited in her religion to sleep with a man unless they commit one of the three actions that were, by the way, asked by God to not do at all when It send them to the earth.

One was not drinking alcohol that they both commit at first, thereby committing the other two which was killing an innocent man, and prostrating to her God, which was just an idol. However, the woman doesn't still sleep with them, and she asks them to tell her the greatest name of God which functions like a password to enter heaven. Nevertheless, God remoulds the woman into planet of Venus forever after she hears the name from Harut and Marut.

[154] Usage of "skirt" as "woman" by Rumi here is not sexist at all despite the opinion of some critics, because according to the story mentioned in previous footnote (153), that woman objectified her body to earn wrong advantage. In addition, "skirt", here, is not used as a general term but used for a specific woman in Harut and Marut story.

We transformed our souls to a slump of disgrace,

  While angels envied us when we first surfaced.[155]

Do you see the depth of this degradation!

  It's even much worse than that skirt's regression.

Mankind's willing horse spanned space all the way through,

  Yet they haven't known the human angels bowed to.

We were born as part of graceful humanity,

  Why are we still branding our vice as majesty?!

How much more of the world are we taking?

  How many more mansions are we making?

If the whole world gets covered with snowflakes,

  To melt them, a day of Sun is all it takes.[156]

With a spark, God can burn all the minister's plots

  And also, the whole confederacies' complots.

God may convert that delusion[157] to providence

  And transform a venom to its curing essence;[158]

It makes that cause of doubt a cause of certitude

  And raises goodwill from the frictions of a feud.

---

[155] Satan was initially an obeying spirit or angel; he was called devil when he objected to the creation of humans thereby rebelling against God according to The Quran and Bible.

[156] Rumi is again criticizing people who get carried away with piling up wealth, and clarifies that everything is very temporary in this world; the same way that snowflakes are when the Sun can easily melt them away.

[157] Delusion of the minister in that he can destroy Christianity

[158] Not only God can change the essence of things, actions and phenomena, but It can as well reverse their qualities so that their essence and effect is completely the opposite of what it was intended to be normally.

The Lord fortified Abraham in a fire,

And made a guardian for spirit from fear.[159]

How God neuters the causes makes me manic;

What his assessments are makes me a cynic.[160]

Minister's Other Craft to Mislead Christians

The minister applied another deception;

He quit his sermons and then prayed in seclusion.

His disciples gradually missed his presence;

They got intolerant of his long absence.

While the isolation was tiring his mood,

They pleaded with him to end his solitude:

"Without you, no light in our life remains;

We are like the blind struggling without canes.

For God's sake, grant us your consideration,

And please halt this unpleasant separation."

"To my fans, my heart still feels dedication,

Yet I must not now conclude this vocation."

Meantime, more fans joined their mournful imploration;

Their primates, too, attended for arbitration:

"What kind of misery is this deprival?

In danger is our spiritual survival.

We are accustomed to your deliverance;

We've fed off the milk of your intelligence.

---

[159] God turned the fear of Abraham from fire into his protection from fire.

[160] It's very interesting that a high-level mystic like Rumi confesses that even he cannot sometimes figure out the purpose or providence behind some events in the world.

Please comfort your zealots and cease this agony.

Don't you pity them for losing your company?

Like ditched fish, they writhe on a meadow.

Open this dam, and let the stream flow!

Oh, there is no one like you around.

Only you can calm our screaming sound!"

Minister Refusing Followers' Imploration

"You are too clung to your ears and my sermons.

Please cut down on your sensory perceptions!

The block to mystic sense is your physique sense.

Mystic ear won't hear till this ear listens.

Dismiss your thinking and all earthly perceptions

So you can hear Its almighty resonance.

Till you're intent on wakeful discourse,

How can you hear the dream in repose?[161]

---

[161] In the last four verses, Rumi is declaring one of the essentials that Sufis, mystics or spirituality fanatics have to pursue in order to deeply perceive the divine presence, and that is minimizing the understanding and thoughts they obtain through their ordinary senses and their daily mental activities.

Even though he is quoting this from the rogue minister's tongue, we have to realize that relying too much on our sensory perceptions and active daily thoughts shut the door on our power of intuitionism (unveiling and intuition as discussed in footnotes 74-75), thereby not deeply perceiving the signals of God. For comparison, Rumi makes an example of a person who is awake and is too intent on his daily mental discourse (active thoughts) but cannot enjoy the beauty of a dream at sleep time. These verses can as well be counted as an indirect encourager of meditation once in a while, as in meditation you have to shut the door on your sensory perceptions.

Our words and deeds are external excursions.

　　The inner excursion is in the heavens.[162]

Made inland, these eyes see their vicinities,

　　Yet the inner Jesus steps on truthful seas.

If inland, the whole lifetime gets wasted,

　　Will a drop of love ever get tasted?

If always in a plain, mountain, or a cave,

　　When are you going to part the ocean wave?[163]

---

[162] Rumi now invites us to have an expedition inside our souls and hearts as humans' words and deeds are just superficial and based on their surface perceptions, and they can hardly reflect the real truth inside our souls. Nevertheless, since our souls are closely connected to our spirits which are themselves connected to the heavens, meditation and contemplation in solitude (inner excursion) can elevate the vibrance of our souls and our inner mystiques.

[163] We need to have the heart to enter the ocean of spirituality to find the meaning of life and reach the highest degree of spirituality like Moses who was able to split the Nile River's wave with God's permission (see footnote 9).

Inland waves involve our grasp, thought, and delusion;

Sea waves have wane, drunkenness and ruination.[164]

Until you're drunken off earthly bliss,

You'll be far from the divine chalice.

Surface talks are like haze clouding the observance;

Heed signs of insight by adapting to silence." [165]

Followers Persistence on Minister Breaking Seclusion

They all responded: "Oh, you sneaky savant!

Please don't treat us with subtlety and torment!

---

[164] Our earthly senses are just limited to our physical peripheries and vicinities; however, our inner mystique (inner Jesus) can expedite our intuition of the infinite cosmos of truth and creation. In Rumi's terminology land is a metaphor of humans' idleness in their worldly and earthly matters, whereas sea and ocean represent the infinite cosmos of truth and meaningfulness that we should get drowned in.

In this verse, Rumi also names the three stages Sufis go through to experience their encounter and unity with the divine spirit:

- First is wane which is the stage Sufis lose their feelings of their own body, and they are so numb to this world, and none of their sensory perceptions give them data of this physical world.

- Second is drunkenness in which Sufis lose their earthly wisdom, and they get so drunk off spiritual love that they are completely unaware of their physical surroundings, and they are very joyous of their spiritual observance of Goddess. Usually, their famous Sama dance happens at this stage.

- Third is ruination or annihilation in which they experience their final unity with the divine spirit as if they are one entity with their Lord.

[165] This couplet is a very important key note by Rumi expressing that not only silence is necessary for receiving divine awareness but we also have to pay very careful heed to divine messages that we can receive during our silence or meditation as those messages can be induced to us at any moment. That tells us we can

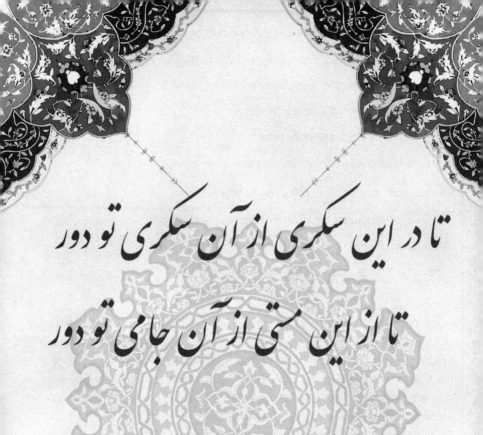

تا در این سکری از آن سکری تو دور

تا از این مستی از آن جامی تو دور

Until you're drunken off earthly bliss

You'll be far from the divine chalice

Load cattle as much as they're able to tackle;

  Charge tasks to the weak as far as they can handle.

Each bird takes a seed that it fits;

  Not all of them can gobble figs.

If a wingless chick flies out of its den,

  It'll be hunted simply by a lion;

But after those powerful wings toughen,

  It can fly miles without lead or burden.[166]

Your words put the devil out of the limelight;

  Your sermons transform our sight into insight.

Having you as the preacher by our side

  Transforms our desert into the seaside.

Without you, our skies don't gleam any light,

  Hence, you're like a moon that brightens our night.

The highness of the firmaments is just optic;

  The highness of the pure psyche is semantic[167].

---

[166] In the follower's reply to the minister, Rumi is implicitly stating that a junior in the spiritual Wayfair will need support and guidance by a senior mystic; nevertheless, once the junior discovers the necessities of mystical knowledge, he can take his expedition further on his own.

[167] Semantic; as in having a conceptual meaning rather than having a physical presence like a matter.

The optical highness may belong to matters;

    The matters beside meanings are like raw letters."[168]

Minister's Response in Refusal of Breaking Seclusion

Please cut short your rationales and thoughts,

    And let my advice flow into your hearts.

If I'm trusted, I may not be blamed

    Even if I say something hare-brained.

If I'm perfect, what's this defiance about,

    And if I'm not, what's this disturbance about?

I won't abandon my hermitage

    As I'm focused on my soul salvage.

Followers' Objection to Minister's Seclusion

They all said: "Sage! This isn't about defiance,

    But it is about the tears of our distance.

---

[168] The soul, psyche, and spirit all are semantic phenomena that have highly valued meanings, and their highness is not visual but spiritual. Matters like skies may have visual or scientific highness, but they don't convey any meanings by themselves. Likewise, matters by themselves compared to these deep meanings are just like some labels and words that without the meanings are just a bunch of letters serving absolutely no value or purpose.

When Infants sob, they don't want to fight their mothers;

They cannot just discern the good of their matters."[169]

We are like a guitar that you neatly plunk;

The chant isn't ours, but it's you playing the song.

We're like the chess pieces in check and mate;

From you, our wins and losses emanate.

O' Lord! You are the dear of all hearts.

Who are we here to have any parts?

---

[169] From the next verse on, it seems that Rumi is poetically praising God by quoting the follower's praise of minister. He is describing one of the highest stages of Sufism or Mysticism, in which Sufis see God as the manager and energizer of all their actions and interactions (not only their existence) in the earthly world, thereby intuitively perceiving Its utter dominance on them and their actions. This stage in Sufism can be translate as "Behavioral Annihilation".

This stage is also the practical part of the concept of "Unity of Being". This principle specifies that all beings we perceive in our universe are actually non-existent and, they are just reflecting the light of the one and only God, or basically everything is the reflection of that one God and there is nothing but God.

Believing in "Unity of Being" though used to be officially known and judged as blasphemous by some earlier clerics, and it used to have death sentence. That's probably why originally Rumi placed these verses immediately after the Christian's response to the Minister. I decided to separate these verses from the Christian's response.

In addition, some Masnavi interpreters specified that these verses could as well be a description of a mood or state, Sufis may experience regarding their masters or senior Sufis as the seniors are the ones who patiently lead the juniors through the difficulties of the spiritual path, so at this stage, they see their master, God, and themselves as one united spirit, and they don't perceive any separation or independence between their own existence and theirs.

We and our instances are of nothingness.

You're the absolute, though you seem fictitious.

We are like lions, but the ones on a banner.

Their attacks are only because of moving air.[170]

Our airs and graces come from your compassion.

Our existence is all from your creation.

You bestowed glee on the inexistent.

You made them love you to a great extent.

O' Lord, please don't retract your favors,

Neither your nibbles, flutes, and liquors.

If you retake them, will you get sought after?

May a painting ever confront its painter?!

Never Mind our sordid presence;

Mind your mercy and magnificence.

We and our demands didn't prevail yet,

When your mercy was having them met.

Portrayals versus the brush and painter

Are like kids, weak and fenced in a venter.

Sometimes God draws a human, sometimes a serpent;

It sometimes may paint contentment, sometimes torment.

No hands may rise to prevent Its drawing;

No words may be said about loss and win.

---

[170] Historically, Iranians used to draw a lion as the symbol of their power on their flags used in their monarch, knight, or army. Rumi uses this Iranian standard of lion, which may seem more majestic when it flows with the help of wind, as the sign of the fake power of humans.

It's not really us that shoot an arrow;

  The archer is the Lord, and we're just the bow.[171]

This isn't about doom and gloom but God's reign;

  Stating Its reign is to learn that we're frail.[172]

Embarrassment hints at volition;

  Frailty insinuates compulsion.[173]

If there was no free will, could there be any shame?

  If there wasn't volition, would there be any blame?

Of our decisions, why do we sometimes back out?

  Or what are education's grading scales about?[174]

Some say: "of their doomed fate, one may be unaware",

  So I ask them to read the following answer. [175]

---

[171] An implication to a verse in Quran: Surah Al-Anfal, verse 17, (8:17), in which God tells Mohammad that actually, the Lord itself is the force behind the arrow he threw in the Badr War: "...you threw not when you throw, but it was Allah..."

[172] Rumi is clarifying in this verse that whatever he mentioned about the Lord's reign over our actions doesn't mean we have absolutely no power over our own actions, but it just means that we are very vulnerable beings besides the Lord.

[173] While the presence of embarrassment after our shameful actions is a hint to the existence of free will or volition, our frailty and flaws are the signs of the presence of compulsion in our lives as due to our weaknesses we may be compelled to do things we don't mean to or don't want to.

[174] If there was no free will, could we punish poor student with low grades or reward the good ones with high grades?!

[175] In the following verses, Rumi is trying to comment on the issue that fatalists raise. Fatalists believe that the shame and regret in humans after their deeds are just because of the unawareness of their predetermined fate.

Frailty and rue occur during sickness;

    Impairment is all about awareness;

Getting impaired, we rue our carelessness;

    Doing wrong, we ask God for forgiveness; [176]

That would unfold for us the vileness of sin,

    And we intend to, henceforth, do the right thing;

We pledge to obey God in our behavior;

    And, that sickness indeed makes us savvier.

O' truth seekers, take heed of this rudiment;

    Those who suffer pain are the ones on the scent;[177]

The more conscious one is in more pain;

    The savvier one's face is more paled.[178]

---

[176] Rumi clarifies that humans feel their frailty and rue when sickness happens to them. During sickness humans also regret their carelessness of not complying with hygiene guidelines. The same way when someone with moral conscience commits a wrongdoing, he regrets his past and gets sick of his mistakes, and realizes how incapable he is. Therefore, Rumi takes this realization of their own incapability or frailty as a sign of awareness arising through humans acknowledging their own inability.

[177] People who suffer from a sickness or pain have sensed some fresh information through intuition that will lead them to more truth about themselves, life, universe, and spirituality.

[178] The more conscious of their surrounding facts a person is, the more pain, frailty, and troubles he has experienced during his life, and likewise the savvier or the more aware of divine truth a person is, the more upset he is as he more deeply realizes the deficiencies and ignorance of people.

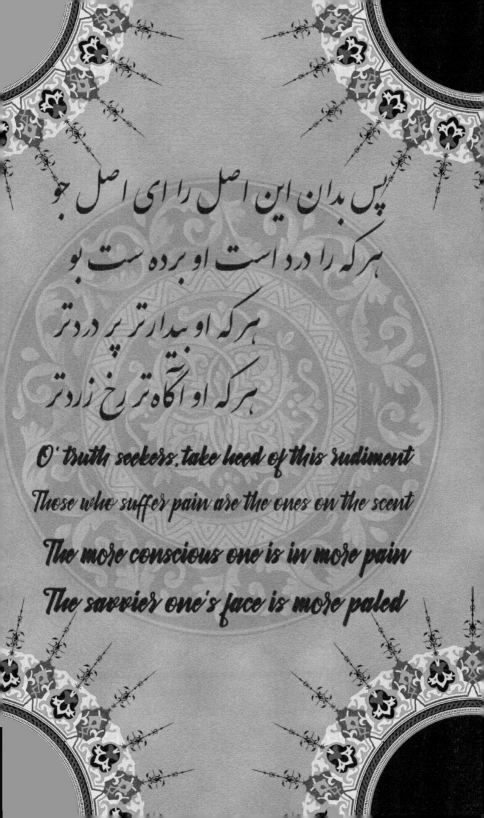

پس بدان این اصل را ای اصل جو

هر که را درد است او برده ست بو

هر که او بیدارتر پر دردتر

هر که او آگاه تر رخ زردتر

O' truth seekers, take heed of this rudiment

Those who suffer pain are the ones on the scent

The more conscious one is in more pain

The savvier one's face is more paled

If you were aware of God's enforced fortuity,

　　Where is its insight and its resulting modesty?[179]

If chained to fate, would we ever rejoice?

　　Does a prisoner always have a choice?

If you feel God's sergeants have made you pent and spent,

　　Don't cow the weak as it's not the trait of the pent.[180]

In what you like to pursue, you sense your own will;

　　In what you hate to ensue, you involve God's drill.

Prophets apply divine fate on the earth;

　　Pagans apply fate to life after death;

Prophets employ free will for life after death;

　　Pagans, though, employ free will for life on earth. [181]

---

[179] Rumi is blaming the fatalists that if they really believe that every event in human life is predetermined by a supernatural power, then why is it that this belief has not given them enough insight to behave more humbly and modestly in their life?

[180] If a fatalist believes his destiny is being confined by God's invisible forces, he should be then humbler with others specially the weak ones as he must be as well feeling the bitterness of being pent and spent by another superior force. Moreover, how can an already-pent and weakened fatalist have the will and power to bully others?

[181] We can conclude, according to Rumi, prophets, saints, or mystics believe in that type of fate in which they relate most part of their success to God's providence and they relate most part of their failure to their own shortcomings rather than fate completely. This way they nor get arrogant because of their success, nor get passive because of their failure. Therefore, they are a type of spiritual or devotee fatalists. This kind of fatalism does have positive effects on human life.

Pagans, on the other hand, blame their wrongdoings on their destiny while taking all the credit for their achievements and they try to earn them though any way possible whether it's the right way or the wrong one.

Every bird flutters towards its own kind;

  The soul's ahead leading its frame behind.

The pagans' souls slumped to the underworld,

  As the earthly joys were what they preferred;

Prophets' souls flew to the empyrean

  For their kind of deeds were ethereal.

There is no end to this discussion,

  So let's go back to the narration.[182]

Minister Fully Dispiriting Followers

Addressing his followers from his hermitage,

  He claimed Jesus had inspired him with this message:

"Stay away from all your friends, relatives, and brood;

  Forget your presence and embrace your solitude."

"After this direction, there should be no debate.

  To bond with the skies, I must calmly meditate.

I'll no longer burn with earthly torments;

  I'll perch by Jesus in the firmaments."

Minister Making Every Primate His Heir Separately

He invoked Christians' primates separately,

  To name them each as his heir deliberately.

He told each: "all others must be your supporters;

  And those who resist must be punished as traitors.

Yet, don't mention this to any other Christian

  Until I'm alive, and don't claim your succession.

---

[182] Rumi implicitly admits that the argument of determinism or fatalism versus free will is a never-ending argument between philosophers.

Here is a scroll of Christ's instructions

That you should read out to all Christians."

He treasured each primate individually,

Giving them scrolls conflicting materially.

Minister's Suicide in Seclusion

After that, he carried on with his seclusion,

And finally committed self-immolation.

When people heard of his final exit,

Crowds went insane by his burial pit.[183]

Christians Asking Primates about Minister's Heir

After a month, the Christians asked their primates:

"Who's the heir, so we can all be his advocates?

Since that sun of wisdom left us in solitary,

We shall seek guidance from another luminary.

The park's rose perished, so before the rest fester,

We shall keep smelling its perfume from rosewater."

As God's greatness doesn't fit in our vicinity,

The prophets were sent as his truthful deputy.

"Deputy" though may not yield the right wisdom

As the boss and deputy aren't a twosome.

---

[183] Rumi might be telling us here that not everyone who the masses go crazy
for is a legitimate and righteous person.

Those, looking just at the surface, see them as split,

But those, looking through things, see them as one unit.[184]

We see two eyes if a face gets looked on,

But the light going through them is just one.

If there were a few lamps in a place,

We may tell them apart by their face;

Whereas, if we pay heed to their radiance,

We won't be able to tell the difference.

We may count as many as apples we want;

However, once we juice them all, they're all one.

No numbers and partitions exist in meanings;

No units and divisions exist in meanings;[185]

The unity of true love and lovers is pleasant;

Stick to meanings as an image may be malignant;[186]

---

[184] In the last two verses and a few following ones, it seems that Rumi is criticizing the externalists, as they have excessive attention on the outward form of religions, thereby neglecting the one and only source of all of them which is the Lord. He also states that the Lord (boss) and his representatives (e.g., prophets) on earth (deputies) are not spiritually and conceptually separate entities, but they are the same. Likewise, Rumi Starts introducing us to the concept of "Unity of Being" which we speculated a bit on in footnote 169.

[185] The incorporeal (like spirits and God), concepts, affections and emotions only have meanings in our mind and they don't have a physical presence, thus it is impossible to divide, count, decompose, and unitize them.

[186] Rumi is inviting us to pay more attention to the meanings of things rather than their sight. For one thing, we may not like what is displayed in some religions, but in fact, they're all conveying the meaning of true love which is God. However, if everyone judges them just on what they see from their surface, matters will get malignant, disruptive and spiteful, and unity and concord become impossible.

Go to pains to burn this malignant image

    To comprehend the unity's advantage;[187]

If you don't burn this wrongful image,

    God will do so with his patronage.[188]

God manifests Itself to breasts.

    It sews the rags of mystic's dress.[189]

We had all been of one expansive essence

    Before we got bound to our fleshly presence;

We sprung from shiny essence like sunshine;

    We had no mess nor knot like Adam's wine;[190]

---

[187] Sufis believe that in order to intuitively enjoy their unification with the Lord, they have to go through some pain of abstinence and self-restraint to dump their ego's desires and judgments, and their mental image of worldly matters.

[188] The Lord has the will to mercifully support the spiritual growth of the human soul (patronage) by manifesting events in human life that make them deeply feel the truth and meaning of life. One of these events is simply death, after which the materialistic vague image made in the human mind is gone and the human soul discerns the real meaning and truth of life which is the spiritual world; however, any other events in human life may lead him to spiritual intuition.

[189] As mentioned in footnote 17, and 102 Sufis used to wear a tattered robe as a symbol of their attention and effort on the non-materialistic and spiritual approach to life. In this couplet, Rumi is metaphorically illustrating how God finally connects (sews) all different dispersed souls, events, and parts (rags) of the universe together to their one unified origin (Sufi's robe), thereby every element or entity or soul returns and connects back to God and discerns the spiritual knowledge.

[190] Our brightening unified spirit (sun) was originally transparent, and without mess or problem (knot) like Adam's wine (water).

As that holy sunshine formed an appearance,

It got countable like shadows of merlons;[191]

Destroy these merlons with a catapult

So that the contrast leaves every adult.

I would elaborate on this; however,

I'm afraid some out of spite would boil over.

These tips are sharp like the tip of sword steel;

Neglect my words if you don't wear a shield![192]

Therefore, I sheathe my sword into its scabbard,

So it won't be misread by any dullard.[193]

---

[191] In the last three verses, Rumi is explicitly describing one of the fundamentals of Sufism or Islamic Mysticism called "Unity of Being". In this theory, God is the only real existence, and everything else is a virtually projected existence of him, and thus not real existence. The existence of God is analogized to the Sun and his creation to sunlight, so as this sunlight projects on the wall of nothingness (us and everything else), it creates all these forms, shapes, and colors of beings we perceive in the universe, or when the sun of God radiates on merlons of a battlement, it creates the shadows of merlons (appearances of the universe as we observe) on the ground (wall of nothingness).

To more deeply understand this subject, imagine the Lord as a projector in a movie theatre that is projecting the picture on the screen (nothingness); the picture is like our universe, and the light is representing God's unstoppable ever-flowing power. "Unity of Being" is one of the major concepts in Sufism, or Islamic Gnosticism and is considered as an extension of the primary principle of Islam which is Monotheism.

[192] "Shield" metaphorically refers to the power of divine knowledge and comprehension that if worn, it helps the reader to intuitively realize Masnavi's keen tips.

[193] The last three verses prove that 'Unity of Being' used to be a very controversial subject.

Primates Controversy over Succession

A primate went to Christians, claiming his succession;

    He showed the scroll proving his title to accession.

Another one came next with the same entitlement;

    Holding his scroll, He provoked the other's resentment.

To the crowd entered all other primates

    While holding swords and title certificates.

Their tribes also brutally attended their scrimmage,

    Causing a lot of beheadings, bloodshed, and carnage.

The skirmish seeds, the minister dispersed,

    In their farmlands, became a deadly pest.

Nuts cracked, and those with hearty kernels in their shells,

    Lusciously flew a pure spirit looking like angels.[194]

Expiration of the flesh is like cracking nuts;

    It will reveal whatever was inside our hearts;

The hearty one turns out sweet like a cupcake;

    The hollow one is all sizzle and no steak;

Whatever's pithy inside will be surfaced;

    Whatever's rotten inside will be shamefaced.

Let's strive hard to discover life's quintessence[195]

    Since quintessence is a wing to appearance;

---

[194] If the human spirit was marked with good traits, deeds, and behaviors during their earthly life, when they pass away (nut cracks), their spirit flying outside of their body will be sublime and majestic (hearty kernel).

[195] Quintessence here is the purest essence and meaning of the universe and all creatures in it or what and why they are meant to be and likewise the spiritual essence of all creatures.

Bond with the lords of spiritual quintessence

   To become gifted and gracious through their brilliance.[196]

The spiritless soul in a cadaver

   Is like a wooden sword[197] in a cover;

Till in the cover, it may have a benefit;

   Once it is out, it is only good for the pit.[198]

Don't take a wooden sword to this encounter[199].

   Carefully check your sword before things fester!

If your sword is wooden, please find another;

   If it's of diamond, go ahead with laughter!

The real sword is in the saints' arsenal;

   Fellowship with them will be phenomenal.

Buy the smiling one If you're buying a nut[200]

   So that the smile reveals the kernel at heart.

---

[196] Rumi is again encouraging us to go around those who have vast spiritual knowledge because they have understood the real meaning and quintessence of life, the universe, and the whole creation.

[197] "Wooden sword" represents a ripe and deficient soul who has not perfected its spiritual growth yet; therefore, he will be unable to perfectly absorb the meaning of life, and will burn and evaporate in the spiritual cosmos.

[198] The souls who have not experienced the spiritual quintessence of life are only worth a bit during their earthly life but worth nothing after death.

[199] Encounter is the battle of life that the human soul faces.

[200] "Smiling nut" means ripe, mature and opened-shell nut representing an honest, decent master and senior in spiritual knowledge.

Sanctified is the profile that with its smile

    Like an open trove, lets out its precious pile! [201]

Unsacred is that tulip's grin

    That barely unveils the dark within.[202]

The mature smiling nut glads the whole garden;

    Friendship with gentlemen makes us gentlemen.

Like a rock, even if we are rough and callous,

    We'll turn into a gem meeting the numinous.

Let the gentleness of saints sit in your heart;

    Only succumb to their love; let the rest part.[203]

There are hopes; don't walk on the streets of distress;

    There are suns[204]; never move towards the darkness.

---

[201] The smile of a senior in spiritual knowledge is an honest sign to his openness and transparency in their vast knowledge; the same way that when a trove opens, it immediately reveals the treasure (spiritual knowledge) inside. In the last two verses and the next verse, Rumi is giving a tip on what kind of master a volunteer of the spiritual path should choose.

[202] A tulip with blackness in the middle represents a deceitful senior and master who are not honest with their spirituality, and they are not open and transparent but hypocritical and deceitful. They probably just use their knowledge to gain power over people, and their bitter indecent smile may hardly lead to identifying the darkness within them.

[203] Rumi warns about the love trap set by deceitful phony mystics who are pretentious and just claim to be friendly and sympathizing.

[204] Sun here represents a luminary who masters spiritual knowledge and the real meaning of life.

The heart drags you toward the numinous;

   The flesh drags you down to a muddy mess.[205]

Feed your heart with communion and affinity;

   From the truly fortunate, seek felicity.[206]

Bible's Tribute to Mohammad

In Bible, the name of Mohammad was mentioned,[207]

   Likewise his qualities and outward description.

A tribe of Christians would honor his stature

   The moment they reached his title in Scripture.

In the skirmish previously cited,

   This tribe came out safe and unaffected.

Their lineage boomed all over their land;

   Mohammad's love gave them a blessing hand.

Others who disregarded Muhammad's name

   Went abject after the minister's shell game.

Their commandments were filled with lots of loopholes

---

[205] Rumi believes if we truly pay heed to the bottom of our heart (as a center of emotions and intuitions), we will be automatically attracted to saints and spiritual sages; however, if we only pay heed to our fleshly and corporal needs, we will be stuck in a swamp.

[206] What our hearts or souls need is the communion and affinity we build with others, especially the true sages of spirituality, mystics. We should also ask them for tips and advice to reach true felicity, not ask others who are drowned in their corporal needs, and not even ask those who are fortunate just wealth-wise.

[207] The Gospels or Bible Rumi is referring to is probably *The Gospel of Barnabas* written by the early Christian adherent, *Barnabas*, who is one of the apostles of Jesus. The name of Muhammad is mentioned in prophecies attributed to Jesus in this Bible.

Following those wilfully conflicting scrolls.

Just quoting his name will escort us that much;

How great his love light would support us as such!

Another Jew King Attempting to Desolate Christianity

After all that incorrigible calamity,

Another Jew King tried to wreck Christianity.

If you're seeking e reference for this matter,

You can refer to the Quran's eighty-fifth chapter.

The wrong custom the first king had based

This other king relentlessly chased.

Whoever founds an ugly practice or fashion,

Only buys himself ongoing malediction.[208]

What's left of a saint is a splendid legacy;

---

[208] It seems like from this verse on, Rumi is implying that entities and phenomena with similar nature attract each other and connect to each other in this universe. For one thing, having a rogue attitude brings about bad events, and people around one's life.

127

What's left of a rogue is curse and inclemency.

For all time, whoever gets a rogue nature

    Like these kings, will tend to grow the same posture.[209]

The saltwater and freshwater are like veins;

    They always find their way into people's brains.[210]

The virtuous have inherited the freshwater.

    The legacy's the Book bequeathed by the Creator.[211]

If you note, the truth-seekers wish for sparkles;

    Sparkles flow from the prophets' gem pinnacles.[212]

Sparkles come to light where the gem glows.

    Sparkles go wherever the gem goes.

---

[209] Bad people will always be around according to Rumi. Anyone who gets accustomed to vile and immorality will eventually develop a rogue character and bothers other people with their dissolute behavior.

[210] Rightness and wickedness in humans' lives will always be current and prevailing like freshwater (representing rightness) and saltwater (representing wickedness). This could mean that at any point in time there will be good and as well wicked people around, or also could mean that any human can be good or wicked depending on his choices.

[211] The virtuous have inherited their freshwater (righteousness) from the prophets, and this righteousness comes from the holy book that God had given to his prophets. This verse has a reference to the Quranic verse in Surah Fatir (35:32) in which God states that we left the holy books as the legacy for the chosen ones (the prophets) but some people ignored its message and did wrong to themselves. Likewise, this verse implicitly states that there is a spiritual connection among all the virtuous and the prophets.

[212] The seekers of truth in the spiritual journey constantly look for tips from the prophets' knowledge, as they are the only ones owning the pinnacle of spiritual knowledge in this world. The luminous spiritual knowledge of the prophets in this verse is represented by the word "gem" and the sparkles are the life-changing tips emitted from this core of spiritual knowledge.

Across the ether, as the Sun travels

   The light through the window as well grovels.[213]

Everyone is connected to a star;

   Their character with that star is on par.

Matched with Venus, they dig love and vivacity;

   Matched with Mars, they seek bloodshed and hostility.[214]

There are other stars beyond this universe.

   They have no extinction and aren't ominous.[215]

They're mobile in the skies but firm under God's rays.

   They're neither attached nor going separate ways.[216]

Those who from these stars acquire their fortunes;

   They burn pagans with their self-confidence.

Their temper won't be moody or Mars-tempered;

   Their ego can't have them rampant or hampered.

---

[213] Again, in the last two verses the core spiritual knowledge of the prophets is compared to luminous objects like a gem or the Sun, and that whoever wants to benefit from this knowledge has to follow this source of light and wisdom; the same way that the light inside a house follows the movement of the sun.

[214] Rumi is cleverly using the science of horoscope and astrology in the last two verses to prove again that creatures with any kind of similarities attract each other. In a way that even the unique position of stars on the time of someone's birth makes an impact on his qualities.

[215] By stars here Rumi is talking about celestial spirits of saints and prophets.

[216] The saints and prophets are like heavenly souls that are mobile and scattered everywhere in the universe, and they are firm and persistent in their divine purpose with the help of God's ever-shining light that separates truth from falsity or obliquity. And even though they are separate souls or individuals (not attached), they are all connected as one unit as they all journeyed the divine path and reached one destination which is divine love.

Their dominant light, safe from dark and frailty,

Is in the grip of God's luminosity.[217]

God showers his light on all spirits;

The fortunate outspread their lappets,

Trying to track down this generous spatter,

Ignoring all the rest but the Creator.

Whoever has got no lappet of devotion

Misses that shower of illumination.[218]

To the universal is particulars' trace.

Nightingales' devotion goes to the flower's face.[219]

Cows are told apart by their skin tone,

But humans by their hearts should be known.

---

[217] The spiritual knowledge (light) of prophets and saints is so bright that illuminates the path for truth seekers and is so perfect that no darkness, evil, and fault gets in the middle of it. However, their perfect light is still in the framework of God's power and dominance and won't do a thing without Its allowance.

[218] In the last three verses, Rumi is again elaborating on the rule of "Attraction of the Similar". The Lord showers his love and blessing on all souls, but these souls have to demonstrate their desire for Its eternal blessings by focusing on divine profusions in the world and spreading their (lappet of) devotion in the universe to attract God's blessings into their lives. Those who don't spread love are only blocking themselves from this generous divine sprinkle.

[219] Every piece (particular) in the universe tends to find its way towards the whole or the universal. For one thing, every drop of water will finally find its way to an ocean. Similarly, pure souls (nightingales) wend their way towards the divine spirit (flower) because it's the holy Lord that they are essentially attracted to.

حق فشاند آن نور را بر جانها
مقبلان بر داشته دامنها

و آن نثار نور را او یافته
روی از غیر خدا برتافته

God showers his light on all spirits
The fortunate outspread their lappets
Trying to track down this generous spatter
Ignoring all the rest but the Creator

Nice tones come out of sincerity dye-tubs;[220]

    Hideous tones come out of cruelty slops;

God's color is the label of that pretty tone;

    God's damnation is the smell of this dirty tone.[221]

Indeed, the drop, traveling ocean to ocean,

    Returns to where it began its expedition.

From Mountains, rivers race down towards the ocean.

    From bodies, the lovely souls rush for devotion.

King Burning Those Not Bowing to His Idol

The king set up a bonfire beside an idol,

    Burning those who don't bow to his absurd symbol.

Since he didn't discipline his ego and selfhood,

    His ego made another idol of falsehood.[222]

Our ego spawns all other idols;

    A dragon that spews snakes for scandals.

---

[220] Another referral to the biblical story of young Jesus in footnote 138, in which sincerity of Jesus and alike is analogized to Jesus' indigo dye-tub in that story.

[221] This verse is also a referral to two verses of the Quran in Surah Al-Baqarah (cow), Verses 138 and 161, (1:138,161) which in one God explains what the color of God is and in the other It explains how damaged the life of pagans, and non-believers will be.

[222] Rumi is analogizing human ego to an idol as humans always try too hard to nurture and satisfy their egoistic desires as if their ego is an idol to worship.

آن چه از دریا به دریا می‌رود ** از همانجا کامد آن جا می‌رود

از سر که سیلهای تیز رو ** وزتن ما جان عشق آمیز رو

INDEED, THE DROP, TRAVELING OCEAN TO OCEAN

RETURNS TO WHERE IT BEGAN ITS EXPEDITION

FROM MOUNTAINS, RIVERS RACE DOWN TOWARDS THE OCEAN

FROM BODIES, THE LOVELY SOULS RUSH FOR DEVOTION

Idol is flame and ego firestarter;

A flame easily gets settled by water;[223]

Water won't ever settle the firestarter;

When will humans get relief from its disaster?

A man-made Idol is sewage in a cartridge;

The ego's, however, the spring of all sewage.

A rock can shatter hundreds of cartridges,

But a spring keeps running streams through the ridges.[224]

While Shattering idols is a piece of cake,

Playing down the ego is a big mistake.

If you are looking for ego formations,

Read about the seven-door nether regions.[225]

By one trick, each ego fools many pharaohs,[226]

Hence into the hands of the Lord, shelter your souls.

---

[223] From this verse on, Rumi analogically explains how human ego is the source of all sins, villainies and disasters in human life. Rumi clarifies that even the idols itself is the creation of human ego and their self-love as they create these false deities to give themselves a sense of fake security by worshiping them.

[224] We may be able to restrict or undermine some egoistic desires (Shattering idols or sewage cartridges). Nevertheless, till the generating source (spring) of egoistic desires is not carefully paid attention to, and is not properly handled, it will keep creating new fleshly desires for us to pursue.

[225] Rumi is referring the reader to the Quranic verse, in surah Al-Hijr, verses 43 and 44, (15:43-44) in which God states there are seven doors to hell. Some Interpret that as seven immoral manners being: gluttony, greed, grudge, anger, lust, and vanity which may all lead to committing sins.

[226] The ego of one person like a pharaoh, or a king can misguide so many other people, who have to abide by them too.

Talking Infant Inciting Others to Jump in Fire

The King brought in a woman with an infant,

    To bow to the idol before getting burnt.

He took the kid away from her and threw in the fire;

    She chose to bow low, seeing the situation dire.

The kid suddenly yelled he was still living

    And asked his beloved mother to dive in,

Saying he's all fine and content

    Though seemingly he's getting burnt.

"This fire is a blindfold masking God's mercy

    As in dawn when the skyline veils lambency.

Enter now to see the Lord's evidence,

    And discern Its elects' exuberance.

Think of this fire as water and enter;

    Leave this world of fire seeming like water.[227]

Join me to find out Abraham's mysteries;

    And how in the fire he found blooms of trees.

While being born, I thought I was close to death.

    I was frightened of falling during my birth.

After I was born, I fled from that tight net[228]

    To breathe the balmy air on this nice planet.

---

[227] Death and martyrdom for God and protecting Its truth seems frightening like fire but in fact, it is as pleasant and pure as water. However, life on the earth as it is, with all its wars, tyrannies, and empty distractions, is like a real fire that is burning the human soul, even though it seems as pleasant as water at first look.

[228] "Tight net" analogically refers to his mother's uterus.

Spiritual Rhymes (On Recognition of Soul & Ego)

Now, I see the earth as the uterus

    As I observed the peace in this furnace.

In this fire, I noticed a universe

    Permeated with the breath of Jesus.

Here is the extinct-looking but self-extant globe;

    There was the extant-looking but fluctuant globe.

Come in that this fire cannot burn anymore;

    Come on as fortune knocks once at every door.

You discerned the abusive power of that clod;

    Get in to see the merciful power of God.

I am inviting you out of mercy solely;

    I have no concern for you as I'm too jolly.

Invite all others too as God's holding a feast;

    And People's feasts can't compete with God's in the least.

All you should fly in like butterflies

    Before this bonanza of springs dies.[229]"

As he was bawling among that cluster,

    Everyone's hearts were laden with luster[230].

Feeling God's love, they began jumping in that blaze

    by Providence, every bitterness turns glazed.

---

[229] Rumi is using "butterfly" here as it is a species willing to change itself. Therefore, here the kid (or in fact Rumi) is inviting us all to embrace the change by taking this opportunity to drop our gluttonous attention and focus on earthly and materialistic life and change or improve our souls by focusing on spiritual life to grow wings like butterflies and take a celestial journey with our new spiritual wings.

[230] "Luster" means glory here.

Shocked by the scene, the officers of the king

    Had to stop them from voluntary burning.

The king then regretfully got downcast

    Since, in their faith, the devout got more steadfast.

The evil ruse boomeranged on that rowdy

    As they got more frank in granting their body. [231]

Mouth Inclination of Who Ridiculed Mohammad

A clown used to mock Mohammad in the hood.

    Once while mocking, his mouth stayed awry for good!

He went to him to get apologetic

    And said: "You're clement and know divine mystique.

My insulting manner was out of lunacy.

    Indeed, I was who deserved that discourtesy."

Should God want to disgrace a person,

    It will tempt them to taunt a godsend.

If God wishes to hide a person's shortfalls,

    It keeps them away from picking others' faults.

---

[231] By this story Rumi is deducting that whenever a person comes up with a guile to oppress others' lives, the universe will outsmart him(her) and backfire at him(her) so that his(her) own life gets unpleasant. This can as well refer to universal law of "attraction of the similar" as in when we commit actions or cause events that impact others' lives in a certain way (good or bad), the universe and our surroundings respond back in the way that we also feel the same certain outcome in our lives.

When God wishes to give us assistance,

> He drags us towards torments and laments.[232]

Joyous is that eye crying for the Lord;

> Merry is that heart frying for the Lord.

We should foresee that after sorrow comes laughter.

> Far-sightedness is a delightful character.

Wherever water flows, it gets verdurous.

> Wherever a tear glows, it fills with kindness.

If you wish for tears, pity those who wail.

> If you need sympathy, back up the frail.[233]

Jew King Blaming Fire

The king confronted the fire to ask with concern:

> "Hey, fiery-tempered one! Aren't you supposed to burn?

Why aren't you burning according to your nature?

> Or was it my tough luck that you lost your feature?"

The fire said: "I'm still the fire with the same nature.

> You're welcome to walk in to test my temperature.

---

[232] Whenever we commit sins and wrong actions in the universe, we face torments, and then we lament our hardship. However, that's a good sign in a way as we have realized our flaws and faults. Therefore, Rumi believes that torments and laments are in fact a divine support that teaches us a lesson so that we don't commit the same mistakes again through life. Hence, that will assist us through our journey to spiritual growth and becoming a better individual.

[233] Rumi believes honest tears from the bottom of the heart is a sign to a soul that after all the hardships and laments it has gone through, it is now more ready and flexible to develop to a higher spiritual level and can understand others' hard times and sympathize with them.

I have not abandoned my burning quality.

I'm a sword that cuts by the rule of Deity.[234]

Guard dogs are welcoming to a familiar face,

But the same dogs jump on strangers at a high pace.

Not any less than a dog, I'm in servitude;

No less than its owner, God deserves gratitude."

When your temper's flame causes you torment,

It burns your soul only by God's consent.

When your nature's flame makes you content,

That content happens by God's consent.

Beg for Its forgiveness if you face torment

As torment is viable by Its consent.

Should God desire, the whole grief swaps with jollity

And all captivities turn into liberty.

Every inanimate object is God's servant.

To us, they may be dead, but for God, they're sentient.

Before God, the fire is always done and dusted[235].

And like a lover, constantly interested.

We rub the steal against the rock for a spark;

No spark, though, will ignite without Its checkmark!

---

[234] In this section, Rumi is explaining the dominance of the Lord over all the phenomena, effects, and features of the earthly world thereby stating that the root cause of all worldly causes and effects that we can observe and perceive is the power of divinity, and should God desire, It can stop the effects of a cause. For one thing, God can stop the burning effect of a fire.

[235] "Done and dusted" means ready to serve

چون خدا خواهد که مانْ یاری کند ** میل ما را جانب زاری کند

ای خنک چشمی که آن گریان اوست ** وی همایون دل که آن بریان اوست

When God wishes to give us assistance

He drags us towards torments and laments

Joyous is that eye crying for the Lord

Merry is that heart frying for the Lord

Don't rub the steal and rock of offense together

'Cause they'll generate you every other bother.[236]

Rock and steel are the cause of the fire,

But let's notice the cause that's higher

For that cause created this cause;

No cause can arise just because!

That high cause that was a guide to a prophet

Is better than those causes in the market [237].

That cause makes these causes effective

But may choose to make them defective.

These causes are familiar to rustic minds;

That cause is familiar to prophetic minds.

What's a cause like? Let's say it can be a cable

That is of use in pulling water from a well;

Yet, the cause of the cable move is the pulley;

Overlooking the pulley spinner is silly.

Don't think that the root cause of all this glory

Is just the cause in the big bang theory;[238]

---

[236] Rumi is metaphorizing the contact of steel and rock generating fire to committing offense to others as it creates a large fire that in its expansion it even burns and bothers the offender.

[237] "The market" analogically refers to today's world, so this couplet basically talks about causes that anyone can distinguish; for example, the cause of rain is cloud.

[238] In Rumi's era, some astronomers (likely atheist ones) believed that the rotation of galaxies in the cosmos is the cause of all phenomena on earth and the whole universe. To make the original verse more contemporary and understandable, the interpreter used the Big Bang theory instead of astronomer's belief in Rumi's time.

Or else, you'll stay hollow and aimless,

    And you'll burn your soul from emptiness.

The wind would douse the fire by God's order,

    While they're both drunken of truth firewater.

The fire of anger or water of patience,

    If you note closely, both stem from Providence.

If the storm's spirit was not aware of God,

    How could it tell apart the bad ones of Aad[239]?

Storm Destroying Aad Tribe in Prophet Hud's Era

Hud drew a line around his faithful laity;

    The storm stalled once it got to their vicinity;

It swept away and brought to naught

    Whoever was out of that spot.

Drawing a magic circle around his cattle,

    Shayban also made sure wolves won't give them hassle!

No wolf was able to cross that marking;

    No sheep could either go out of the ring.

The halo of a saint would impede

    The storm of the sheep's greed and wolves' greed.

---

[239] Aad is an ancient tribe mentioned frequently in the Quran. According to the Quran, they were a prosperous nation who started committing sins and crimes very extensively, so God sent a prophet, called *Hud*, among them to guide them to truth and goodness. However, they made fun of the prophet and arrogantly continued their offending manners. Hence, the Lord destroyed their whole tribe except those who believed in God with devastating storms.

این رسنهای سبها در جهان

هان و هان زین چرخ سرگردان مدان

تا نمانی صفر و سرگردان چو چرخ

تا نسوزی تو نر بی‌مغزی چو مرخ

Don't think
that the root cause of all this glory

Is just the cause in the big bang theory

Or else
you'll stay hollow and aimless

And you'll burn your soul from emptiness

For the saints likewise, the storm of death

    Gently glides through like a fragrant breath.

In the fire, Abraham wasn't burnt

    As he was God's chosen servant.

The pious don't burn from the fire of lust

    While it takes the rest down past the earth's crust![240]

Since the sea waves move only with the Lord's orders,

    They didn't drown Moses' folks with pharaoh's soldiers.[241]

Once the order of the Lord reached the earth,

    It buried Korah[242] with all of his wealth.

Once the clay sniffed the Jesus' sigh,

    It grew wings and flew to the sky.[243]

Our hallelujahs are zephyrs out of clays[244]

    Becoming heaven birds out of hearts' pure praise.

Mount Sinai swayed after absorbing the Lord's light

    And lost all its flaws to be a mystic outright.

---

[240] The damaging effect of lust in humans is compared to the fire as it affects human's judgement and perception by taking over their mind and decisions.

[241] Revisit footnote 163 for more info.

[242] Korah was a super wealthy individual during Moses' era who is known for leading a rebellion against Moses and his name and story was mentioned in Book of Numbers of the Hebrew Bible and Surah Al-Qasas of The Quran (28:76-84).

[243] One of Jesus' miracles, as mentioned in both Bible and The Quran (Surah Al-'Imran, 3:49) was that he would breathe into clays and turn them into sparrows.

[244] The substance of the human body

A mount being a mystic shouldn't be of surprise

    Because Moses' substance was out of clay likewise.

King's Ironic Denial and Rejection of Nobles' Advice

Even though the Jew king witnessed all that marvel,

    By using tart words, he phrased his disapproval.

Advisors proposed he stop his opposition.

    Yet, he arrested them and threw them in prison.

Because he overdid his tyranny,

    God ordered the start of his agony.

Then God ignited a flame of fire

    That encircled those jews going haywire.

Their roots were out of fire initially;

    They went towards it eventually;

They were sparks thrown off from a fiery source;

    To the whole, each segment follows its course.[245]

They tried to scorch those in their faith steadfast,

    But it was them who got blackened at last.

Whoever the underworld has been their base,

    The underworld[246] will be their eternal place.

---

[245] The way of particulars (segments) is towards the universal (whole) - A philosophic statement that Rumi uses a lot throughout Masnavi. For more illustration see footnote 219.

[246] The former appearance of "underworld" in this verse means "world of crime", but the latter means hell as criminals' and oppressors' souls in the end will fall to this underworld, as crime and tyranny was the base of their deeds and behaviors. It seems that by this verse Rumi is referring to quranic verses in Surah Al-Qaria (101:8-11) in which it declares that the souls of those whose weight of deeds are low (so many bad deeds but just a little or no good ones) will drop to the depth of the underworld.

A mother looks after her brood;

    Branches are followed by their root.[247]

Although the water in a pool looks imprisoned,

    The wind soaks it up and carries it in the end;

The wind lets it out and takes it back to its source

    So gently that no one notes this matter-of-course.[248]

Likewise, gradually by every breath,

    Our lives get stolen from the cage of earth.

Our upright breaths and prayers rise to the beyond;

    To the next life, with them, we supply a trust fund.

Then God will return us Its divine plaudits,

    So we further transcend our spiritual limits.

This telepathy keeps going through this cycle

    Until the soul reaches its mystic pinnacle.

Our appetite derives from food flavor;

    That allure stems from tasting God's favor.

Humankind has eyes for a direction

    That has already once touched their passion.

---

[247] The same way that there is a tendency between kids and their mother, there is likewise always a tendency between sinners and hell. Kids always go back to their mother at the end of the day and the mother always look after them; the same way sinners always do things to connect themselves to hell, as if the hell always looks after them. Therefore, each sinner soul is like a branch derived from their root of hell.

[248] The sun evaporates the pool water, and the wind gradually takes its evaporated drops back to the ocean through clouds and rain. The keyword, here, is "gradually"; therefore, how we can interpret these verses according to the context is that if God wants to punish the sinners, and offenders, he may do so very gradually that not only people but even also themselves will not notice it.

Each kind's zeal springs from its own variety;

    Each segment's passion stems from its entirety;

Or if a thing's apt to be one of the kinds,

    It becomes of that kind once to that it binds;

For one thing, food and water aren't of any kind,

    But they're added to our kind once to us they bind. [249]

Due to food's final effect, count it as a breed,

    Although it can't have the role of a breed indeed.

If our zeal is stemmed out of things, not of any kind,

    It's just similar to a congruous kind in mind;

Whatever similar is just a loan,

    And a loan is not there forever to own.

Birds may fall for the zeal of a fake twitter[250];

    Then they see no mate but only disaster.

---

[249] Rumi categorizes the ongoing attractions in the universe to three main classes:

- The attractions occurring between species of the same kind like the ones between a man and a woman, or between two birds. In spiritual context, this means that two souls who are well-mannered or virtuous will attract each other, or the attraction rising between two rogues or criminals.
- The attractions of segments, pieces, or particles to their whole or entirety like the tendency of every water drop to finally reach its source which is ocean or like the eventual return of all souls and spirits to the main spirit which is the Lord.
- The third (mentioned in the next verse) is the materials potential to join a kind by getting absorbed into a species. Water, food and alike are examples of this type of attraction or absorption. The spiritual example of this type is when a neutral soul capable of spiritual growth gets drawn toward a virtuous personality.

[250] Bird call or fake tweet sound that bird-hunters use to lure birds

A mirage for the thirsty is a glitter

    That once they reach, they escape to seek water.

From Kalila[251], let's retrieve the next fable,

    And extract lessons that are much cerebral,

So that avarice doesn't put you on the wrong track,

    And wrong ideas don't cause you a huge setback.[252]

---

[251] Kalila is short for Kalila-wa-Dimna is an ancient Indian book consisting of fables conveying morals.

[252] To prevent our world from wrong ideas and their setbacks, please rate and review this book on the website you bought it from if you have liked the teachings of "English Rumi" so far.

To be continued...